The Generations of Adam

This impassioned and original book is an exploration of stories – personal stories, family stories, allegories, histories, myths – and of one myth in particular: the Genesis account of creation. Eric Rhode takes the Genesis narrative and inter-weaves it with others: with *Paradise Lost,* with the wanderings of King Lear, with Piero della Francesca's painting of the Nativity, with Bunyan's listening in to a group of women as they sat 'at a door in the sun', talking about a new birth.

This is not ordinary story-telling. It is autobiographical writing against the grain. Rhode calls it a form of anti-autobiography. He suggests that our need for meaningful stories may blind us to the fact that truth of its nature does not always take symbolic forms. Rhode's re-telling of the story of Adam becomes an exploration of proto-mental states, in which tales can exist that need no tellers.

Eric Rhode, formerly a broadcaster and film critic, is a psychotherapist in private practice. He is the author of *Tower of Babel: Speculations on the Cinema* (1966), *A History of the Cinema* (1976) and *On Birth and Madness* (1987).

GW00568316

The Generations of Adam

Eric Rhode

'an association in which the free development of each
is the condition of the free development of all'

Free Association Books / London / 1990

First published in Great Britain in 1990 by
Free Association Books
26 Freegrove Road
London N7 9RQ

British Library Cataloguing in Publication Data
Rhode, Eric, 1934–
    The generations of Adam.
    1. Thought processes
    I. Title
    153.42

    ISBN 1–85343–130–3 hb
    ISBN 1–85343–131–1 pb

Typeset by MC Typeset Ltd, Gillingham, Kent

Printed and bound in Great Britain

For Jocelyn and Richard

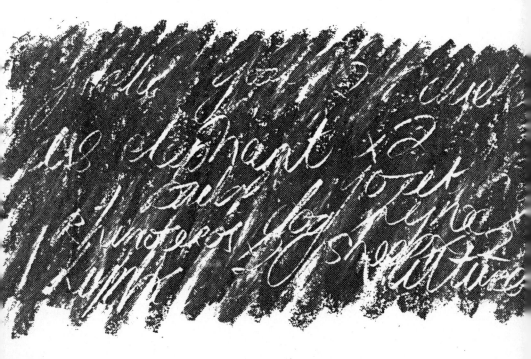

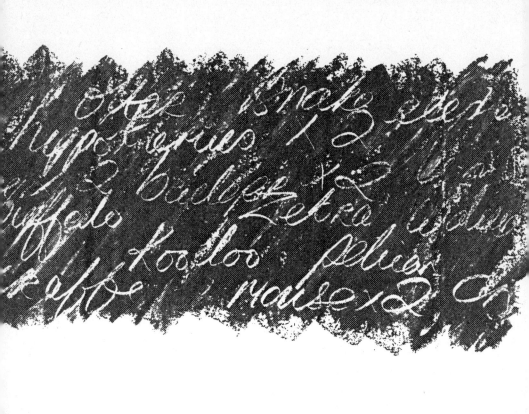

Some Divines count Adam 30 *years old at his creation because they suppose him created in the perfect age and stature of man . . .*

Sir Thomas Browne, Religio Medici

To find no contradiction in the union of old and new, to contemplate the Ancient of Days and all his works with feelings as fresh as if all had then sprang forth at the first creative fiat, characterizes the mind that feels the riddle of the world and may help to unravel it. To carry on the feelings of childhood into the powers of manhood . . . this is the character and privilege of genius . . .

Samuel Taylor Coleridge,
Biographia Literaria

Assertion always implies a denial of something else. Stop to think of it, and it has flown! What the world was to Adam on the day he opened his eyes to it, before he had drawn any distinctions, or had become conscious of his own existence – that is first, present, immediate, fresh and initiative, original, spontaneous, free, vivid, conscious and evanescent. Only, remember, that every description of it must be false to it.

C. S. Peirce, 'A guess at the riddle'

Sir Thomas Browne: . . . *we carry with us the wonders we seek without us: that is all Africa and her prodigies in us; we are that bold and adventurous piece of nature, which he that studies, wisely learns in compendium, what others labour at in a divided piece and endless volume.*

Coleridge (commenting): *This is the true characteristic of Genius — our destiny & instinct is to unriddle the world, & he is the man of Genius who feels this instinct fresh and strong in his nature — who perceives the riddle & the mystery of all things even the commonest & needs no strange and out of the way Tales or Images to stimulate him into wonder & a deep interest.*

Samuel Taylor Coleridge, Marginalia

Contents

Acknowledgements

I should like to thank Karl Figlio, Miranda Chaytor and Bob Young at Free Association Books for their help.

The author and publishers would like to thank the following for permission to quote from published material: Faber & Faber Ltd and the Estate of T. S. Eliot for extracts from T. S. Eliot, *Four Quartets*; Laurence Pollinger Ltd and the Estate of Mrs Frieda Lawrence Ravagli for extracts from H. T. Moore, ed., *The Collected Letters of D. H. Lawrence*, and from Aldous Huxley, ed., *D. H. Lawrence. Letters*, selected by Richard Aldington; and Jonathan Cape Ltd for an extract from Claude Lévi-Strauss, *The Raw and the Cooked*.

Part I

1

A form of anti-autobiography

ANYONE MIGHT ask the question: what is the meaning of my life? How (if at all) may I contemplate my life, as though from outside myself?

Questions of this kind preoccupy people in therapy, in much the same way as they used to preoccupy people in Tolstoy's novels. I remember a patient who dreamt of travelling by boat down a river. The opening out of the vista in his description invited the feeling that the whole of life was unfolding within the span of a journey. The more you looked, the more you saw, within some expanding conception of the imaginative vision.

But therapeutic uses of the imagination of this kind are infrequent. To use thought in this way, you have to assume a certain kind of literacy, at some distance from the more fundamental processes of development. Many people in therapy sink into a torpidity of the soul, states in which they find themselves confused and lost in a multitude of particulars; they would seem to be remote from any alertness to general contexts, having moved (it would seem) close to the sources of symbol formation, states of mind that are pre-literate, pre-verbal and possibly pre-human.

It is important, since I cannot directly know these states, to have a myth about them – and the myth that occurs to me is one concerning the foetus, as I imagine it, in some intuitive communion with its uterine surroundings. I think of the foetus as having the capacity to be inspired without having to enter into a process of learning. Goodness filters into it; it tunes in and, without any form of mediation, it receives. This is to find a setting in which a belief in wish fulfilments is appropriate.

I was made aware of this likeness to a vegetable growth in my own self when in psychoanalysis, and then more comfortably when I began to observe interactions between infants and mothers, and much later when I had the opportunity to work with a seriously incapacitated child. Previously, I had looked to different norms: an Everyman model, or Adam, who happened to be endowed with the faculties of a bright university graduate; someone who lives off his wits, dissociated from any acknowledgement of the dependent or helpless elements in the self. Such a conception of mind, which tends to think of powers of speech as much superior to other forms of symbolization, is hard to maintain and can lead to breakdown. It is a conception of mind that at one time (I think) was quite widely held.

The eminent American painter, Barnett Newman, once contended that the first man must have been an artist. It is unlikely that Newman thought that the first man had grown into being an artist or had been nurtured into receptivity; since growth of this kind supposes sponsors, like parents or animals, who might have helped the infant Adam grow. For me Newman's poetic assertion suggests someone isolated, lonely and mature in his acts of receptivity, a new man like Newman himself.

If Newman did in fact follow Genesis and believe the first man to have sprung into being as an artist fully formed, he would have found his idea reflected in Sir Thomas Browne.

4

'Some Divines,' argued Browne, 'count *Adam* 30 years old at his creation because they suppose him created in the perfect age and stature of man' (Browne, 1643, p. 88). This is a conception of mind in which the power to apprehend the numinous, or to symbolize, are God-givens in human nature rather than achievements acquired through nurture and training. Adam is born an artist; he does not have to grow into the aptitudes and skills that the artist requires. He does not have to pass through states of incoherence to recognize the elements of pre-verbal wisdom in intuition.

In unsettled times, or times when the traditions of nurture seem inappropriate, myths of this kind are important. I need to believe that I can tune into inspirations which my miserable surroundings do not supply me with. Talent (and Newman was hugely talented) requires a precedent for its moments of originality. Why, imitating tribal thought, should talent not look for its precedent to the unknowable and mythic first moment of Creation itself? 'The primary Imagination,' wrote Coleridge in the *Biographia Literaria*, is 'a repetition in the finite mind of the eternal act of creation in the infinite I AM' (Coleridge, 1817, p. 167). A creationist myth of this kind is inimical to theories of nurture and symbol development: it is anti-historical, anti-familial and anti-cultural; and it is inclined to value art because it is (as Freud thought) primary process, a kind of sacred magic.

Newman and certain other non-figurative artists of the 1940s sought a tradition in tribal and palaeolithic art, sources largely unknowable in origin, that could be co-ordinated with the exploration of unknown goals. Against common opinion, they believed that primitive thought represented states of consciousness higher than those in the culture they inhabited.[1]

Newman's theory is informative of a whole range of intuition and prejudice in our culture concerning the nature of inspiration. It informs thinking about the arts, at least about art since the time of Cézanne. Discussing the nature of the motif with Joachim Gasquet, Cézanne said that he looked for inspiration to the first artists, the cave painters, as an antidote to post-classical facility. He wanted to paint naïvely, to recover a primitive vision. He was willing to enter into states similar to psychosis, of turbulent infantile disablement, as a necessary part of the process by which he reached out for meaning – for what he called the motive or motif.

In other words, if Adam or the essential self is to be an artist, he needs to be able to experience conditions of regression, which of their nature suppose the continuance of the dimensions of infancy within the adult self (though logically, I suppose, Adam the artist might have these dimensions without having actually passed historically through infancy itself). Within the dimensions of infancy, the artist experiences not only the processes of symbol formation but also failures in symbol birth, Coleridgean despondencies, aberrations and abortions. He may also experience a strong trend in mind towards the anti-symbolic: to obduracies in thought, among which he may include the irreducible presence of Platonic ideas or the God of Genesis.

Genesis, in fact, gives some sort of support to this idea. The artist in the self, lonely in a culture which at times resembles a polluted Eden, finds his reflection in Adam. God grants Adam the right to name the animals – more specifically, in certain much later versions of the myth, God grants Adam the right to name the animals to relieve him from the depressing condition of celibate loneliness. Naming, like the Orphic music which tames the beasts, curbs the animal within as well as the actual beast without and draws them both into the human sphere. It is possible that through acts of naming, Adam acquired the power to understand an animal lore otherwise inaccessible to humans. (Practitioners of magic surely take on animals as familiars to acquire this lore.)[2]

In the beginning, the world did not centre on man. It was not man, after all, who said *fiat lux*. Nor did the world centre on itself (as I think is implied by some of the early nineteenth-century geologists). Everything centred on a God mysterious in intention. Animal, vegetable and divine rationality were undifferentiated and existed within a ground that was wholly divine. I conjecture – although this is not in Genesis – that Adam's acts of naming can be seen as an attempt to recover the primary unity – its being, literally, a Platonic re-collection. To this extent it is a failure, since Adam continues to ache in emptiness. God creates Eve; presumably, in another bid to save Adam from depression. Creating Eve is the boldest pre-Fall attempt to recover some dreamt-of unity in the cosmos.

Eloquent through God's gift, Adam becomes able to acknowledge the sacred particularities of animal creation. He anticipates the encyclopaedia-makers. But his ability to talk does not emerge out of some germinatory state of pre-speech. He cannot be thought to have passed, as Aristotle thought the foetus to have passed, through vegetable and animal states, in identification with conditions that may or may not know consciousness.

In such an Adam I find a model for the Renaissance type of magus who sought, extraordinarily, to describe a creation which he wished to rise above and to hold at some distance from himself. A bachelor's loneliness becomes a bachelor's loftiness, splendid in its way but too remote to engage creatively with anything. In Michelangelo and Milton, Adam is born a Renaissance hero and humanist scholar; innately perfect in a cosmos that bears whatever signs of imperfection may need to be borne. Such an Adam continues to be an influential model in our culture.

This is not the prototype I turn to in psychotherapeutic experience. The world of the born is made up of categories usually (as in the case of sexual genderings) based on the biological inheritance and on often cruel discriminations. But in the realm of the unborn, of potentialities realizable or denied, we all find a common Adamic inheritance wider than the Renaissance conception of Adam. As I try to show in later chapters of this book, the idea of an Adamic inheritance may derive from some pre-birth recall of the unusual and fabulous condition of the uterus. I see no reason why my Adam should not be an embryo capable of wonder, or a brain-damaged child, or the absence where a foetus might have been. It is to such an Adam that I look to as a primary model for human nature. My Adam lives in realms of intuition and magic. He may feel truth to pour into him as sunshine pours into the basin of a fountain, but he will never know the concept of hallucination (which I hope to demonstrate is a post-natal concept). He is a Caliban perhaps, someone who in imagination continues to exist *in utero*. I recognize that I derive in part from this prototypic Adam-father.

Aquinas proposed a theory of knowledge that depends on an idea of a God who can contemplate and grieve over those imaginary beings who will never be born, those who are beyond human conception as well as those who are unconceived: beings who exist beyond the human imagination but who are real for God.[3]

To believe in a mind unlimited by human theories of potentiality and capable of meditating on sources of life outside the human understanding enriches the thinking of the psychotherapist. It encourages a certain scepticism concerning psychiatric descriptions. Those who cannot speak take on the presence of important witnesses; and the words on the tongue of the psychotherapist begin to change.

I assume that creationist myths are substrates to conscious thought, ways of holding together possibilities and of marking out the unknowable. (Many Victorians felt destroyed when they were not allowed a meaningful relationship to these myths.) When I think of the Genesis Adam, I realize that this substrate is an unavoidable contract, which binds Adam and the future generations of Adam to the first fiat – a contract which I cannot wish away without losing everything. In this world I am locked into a perfection which I cannot deny without destroying myself; a perfection which finds its appropriate myth in the God who re-creates the world at every moment.[4]

Notes

1 Kirk Varnedoe has written of them:

> This emphasis on collective truths that were timeless/psychic rather than historical/social matched and supported claims for a new 'apolitical' artistic individuality. The modern artist's unconscious was held to be a direct link to a living well of collective memory, and difficult, apparently non-communicative modernist abstraction was argued to be the true embodiment of eternal communal verities. (Rubin, 1984, p. 619)

Cf. Barnett Newman: 'Shall we say that modern man has lost the ability to think on so high a level?'

2 'The prestige of animals in the eyes of the "primitive" is very considerable; they know the secrets of Life and Nature, they even know the secrets of longevity and immortality' (Eliade, 1957, p. 63; and see pp. 59–72). Also cf. the fascinating discussion in Lovejoy and Boas, concerning the cult of animalitarianism, the belief associated with certain forms of primitivism that many animals represent a form of life higher than those of the human. (Lovejoy and Boas, 1935, pp. 19–22).

3 'Other things there are which can be produced by God or by creatures, yet are not, were not, and never will be. With respect to these God is said to have not knowledge of vision, but knowledge of simple understanding' (Aquinas, 1964, p. 33).

4 Is the mind of the creationist Adam who sprang into being in full maturity relatable as a type to theories of development? In one sense, yes. There are two differing stories in Genesis concerning the creation of Eve. In the second story, Adam seems complete, but God indicates an inadequacy. 'And the Lord God said, It is not good that the man should be alone. I will make a help meet for him' (Genesis 2:18). Is Adam lonely? We do not know. Genesis does not describe psychological states; and whether Adam had a mind or not is not given. God creates the animals and then Eve. At this point, development of a biological, mental, cultural kind may be supposed to begin.

The pre-developmental aloneness and creation of Eve was elaborated on by the Romantic poets who were fascinated by Milton's psychological description of aloneness as 'Adam's ache'. Keats saw the story of Eve's creation in terms of Adam's thoughts while asleep, a moment of pre-development vision or apocalypse which Keats uses as a model for a Romantic conception of the Imaginative.

Mind as a source for development and mind as a receptor of inconsequential poetic vision are two separate and indeed conflicting understandings of mind, a most useful idea for anyone who wishes to investigate the origins of symbolism. Certainly the idea of someone being born fully fledged at the age of thirty and opening their eyes on an adequate world is a wonderful image for revelation as a knowledge that is not acquired through nurture or training.

2

Psychotic literalism

IN THE National Gallery in London, beside Piero della Francesca's painting of the Nativity, there is a small notice, informing the spectator that Piero painted this picture with failing sight. Piero was unable to complete the picture because he went blind.

I was, and continue to be, moved by this observation. That Piero should use his dying sight to record his vision of a hallowed infant – of a birth representing the miracle of all births – and that his translucent vision should live up to the promise of the subject, has become an enduring part of my imaginative history. It nourishes me in a way that only an imaginative fact can do.

I learn that the small notice is probably in error. Piero did not go blind. The ground gives way beneath my feet: I think myself cheated. And yet the imaginative fact of Piero's going blind continues to live within me and to move me. I continue to maintain the importance of imaginative history – the history of indelible happenings in the mind – as against the history of possible facts.

In thinking about this experience, I remember that I have both neurotic and psychotic dispositions in myself.

From the neurotic viewpoint, I assert that imaginative information, though factually false, is myth. Since I (as a neurotic) do not take myths literally, as demonstrable truths, nor wholly think of them as lies, I am able to equivocate my position in a characteristically neurotic fashion. Myths communicate truth in feeling, but in an ambiguous fashion. They are metaphoric in structure. Their meanings are translatable – and once meanings are translatable, there is no holding the translator. For instance, I could argue that the myth of Piero's failing sight moves me because I sense that this is how an artist continues to be true to his good objects, even at the moment of their leaving him. This translation is unlike the literalism, and the adhesion of the image in Piero's dying eyes: the inevitability in revelation of certain kinds of art; the wish to make in art something as irrefutable in the completeness of its structure as the world created by the Genesis God.

I make the other move: admit psychosis, and take the myth literally – see metaphors as disjunctive assertions and deny place in my mind for ambiguity, hypothesis, or equivocation. I will deny the realm of fiction and the right to say 'To be or not to be'. I will be given over to a dimension, in which dreaming and waking thoughts, or hallucinations and revelations, are indistinguishable. Whatever exists in my mind, in the psychotic dimension, is the actual world. A lie or factual error, even a deliberate lie, becomes the truth.

The neurotic does not really believe in myths; nor does he really believe in his having a mind. He uses both myth and mind expediently. He does not believe in them. Untruths and incredible configurations move him, and cannot be lived without; he may think of these doubtful entities as art and give them the precarious status of myths – by which he means, in neurotic terms, a lie that is socially acceptable.

He does not think of myth as the psychotic self thinks of myth – as truth itself. He lives in doubt; equivocates; thinks of the actual world and the myth world as parts of a

metaphor, between whose parts he glides. Santayana's picture of man in general applies to the neurotic in particular.
The neurotic 'has a prejudice against himself: anything which
is a product of his mind seems to him to be unreal or
comparatively insignificant' (Santayana, 1896, p. 3).

The psychotic self will have none of this: the content of
mind – by being in this mind rather than any other mind – is
the prime reality. The psychotic can claim to have absolute
access to the contents of mind and to dogmatize belief. He
sees myths as God's Word that must be read literally. His
mind is the whole world, and the totality of its existence
cannot be refuted; and yet God made the separate world
which unfolds before his psychotic mind. Sometimes he
painfully wonders whether God might be someone other than
himself.

The fact that I am moved by the opening chapters of
Genesis and by the play, *King Lear*, allows the tentative,
Hamlet-ish, metaphor-prone neurotic in me to claim that
they are stepping-stones in the development of my mind –
important events in my imaginative history. They mean
something to me in a way that the rise and fall of kings does
not. The only history that matters is a history of the heart:
and what happens to me in my mind is as irrefutable as God's
first fiat. The psychotic says: they are, in fact, identical.

The neurotic thinks he knows the object of his love. It is as
he desires it: fluid, ambiguous and tentative. It sows doubt in
the desire itself for love. I can read and re-read the text in
many ways; it can be reviewed by others; scholars may
emend it. The love object of the neurotic disappears in a
cloud of scrupulous conjectures.[1]

The psychotic self disagrees. There is only one irrefutable
love: the love of God for man, proclaimed at every point in
the universe. What is there, in my mind, must be true. The
invisible marks my mind in a literal fashion and bears witness
to itself in ways that I cannot forget. For the psychotic, there
is nothing tentative or wayward about these markings; they
are absolute, the markings of God. The lightest of them

carries the authority of the entire universe. Our most intimate moment, the moment when we are most privately in ourselves, glows with universal lights.

The psychotic in me says: Genesis and *King Lear* are fundamental facts in my mind, comparable to the anecdotes my sea-faring grandfather used to tell me or the silences of my father. The only true text of Genesis and *King Lear* that matters is the first text that I read and that deeply moved me and that has indelibly marked me. The indelible markings on my heart, that no post-mortem will reveal, are the only truth: this is identical to the world at its first creation.

But what if the objects that made the marks did not exist, if I had been deluded, if I had been hallucinated? These are *Hamlet* questions, and the psychotic ignores them. He distrusts metaphors and the circuities of symbolism. He distrusts myths as other than a literalism.

In order to survive, goodness must conceal itself, as Edgar in *King Lear* painfully learnt: the waiting is all. 'The dark and vicious place where he thee got/Cost him his eyes' (V. iii. 164). Goodness is Edgar disguised, Christ as infant veiled, Moses in the bullrushes. Who dares look on the Nativity – any nativity?

What did Piero see with his failing eyes? I presume: a vision (literal in content) of the hallowed child. Piero did not see a metaphor for inner states. He did not see a myth – in the sense of a narrative which conjectures mental states. He saw nothing. Tentative marks on a patchy surface: incomplete Piero masterpiece, masterpiece through its incompleteness, bearing the authority of a fundamentalist text.[2]

To acknowledge the psychotic part of the self is to acknowledge that something metaphoric is given to you literally: neither the something, nor the giver of the something, can be demonstrated in a court of law. In the court of law it will be assumed that the psychotic has created the giver and the gift in his own head (which in fact may be the case; as in the case of the man who thought his eyes were film projectors unspooling the world before him). It may even be assumed that all religious formulations are a species of hallucination, and that God, the giver of revelations, is no more than a manner of speaking.

Bottom's dream

An infant dreams of its mother's breast. It is convinced that it has fed at this breast. It is unable to differentiate dream from an actual experience. Did it actually feed or did it only dream the feed? Like Piero, ravished by revelation, it does not think it might pine through undernourishment. It finds itself unable to differentiate one mode of sense communication from another.

It communicates incoherence in a way that amuses its superior brothers and sisters. 'The eye of man hath not heard, the ear of man hath not seen, man's hand is not able to taste, his tongue to conceive, nor his heart to report, what my dream was' (*A Midsummer Night's Dream*, IV. i. 210). In *A Midsummer Night's Dream*, revelation induces incoherence in Bottom. The meanings of revelation must be equivocated in order to be tolerated. The comicality of the mechanics in both rehearsal and performance resembles the toddler in the nursery play, accommodating itself to untolerated vision.

The little donkey-infant was loved by its spiritual mother, Titania. Only jealous Puck and Oberon think it under a spell. Theseus, who tolerates the psychotic excesses of the imagination, believes we should attend to incoherence. Love and tongue-tied simplicity, he thinks, 'in least speak most.'

Consider Bottom as the changeling child who finds its mother in both Titania and Titania's pregnant friend, the vot'ress, who died in childbirth. In a different play Bottom re-appears as despised Caliban, child of blue-eyed Sycorax, blue-eyed through being pregnant,[3] one of the most loathed presences in the Shakespeare canon, perhaps because she was beautiful in pregnancy. Caliban's dream is a variant on Bottom's dream:

in dreaming,
The clouds, methought, would open, and show riches

Ready to drop upon me; that, when I wak'd
I cried to dream again.

(*The Tempest* III. ii. 143–6)

'The dark and vicious place where he thee got/Cost him his eyes'. I look at the world, at the sky, in its irrefutable completeness. Either it, or I, must go: there can be no place for both of us. The moment of sensing the otherness of futurity destroys eyes.

Ruskin

Ruskin in dotage, on the arm of a housekeeper, attends a Rembrandt exhibition. Proust describes him: 'He had blear eyes, a doting expression – such extraordinary beings they are, the aged or the sick, who already look like the dead or idiots, and in whom we now discover, violently manifested by a shaky arthritic hand, that amazing will-power which disconcerts a whole family' (Proust, 1958, p. 255). Piero's blindness once more: we are invited into thinking the moment true. But the description is imaginary; so far as we know Ruskin did not attend the Rembrandt exhibition. Proust made it up. The intensity of the creativity in the painting appears to intensify Ruskin's frailty. Piero was inspired by extremes of authority: the frail helplessness of an infant who he assumed incarnated an absolute God. In a similar way, Rembrandt drew an almost supernatural life from the sight of ancient beings. The helpless who endure, the foetus in the infant, inspires the adult self. It would seem to know all that I am left to know: knowledge that I hope to retrieve when I am dying.

Ruskin, in Proust's portrait, might be a Rembrandt subject. It is as though Proust were vying with Rembrandt in his sumptuous description of helplessness: both had known this helplessness in infancy, both might renew its acquaintance in an imagined old age. Proust is tentative, neurotic, inviting his reader to read facts as possibilities, eventually casting doubt on the existence of actual facts in a mind given over to possibilities: an imaginary Ruskin attends an actual Rembrandt exhibition; an actual Ruskin studies Rembrandt's works of the imagination. What is not directly given is the schismatic body-blow of psychotic vision, the moment of death-in-life and life-in-death.

Dying monk

A Tibetan monk, who believed in transmigrations of the spirit, was able to give a moment-by-moment account of his changing states of consciousness as he died. His self-esteem was related to his detachment: his ability to conduct scientific observation – even under circumstances that would eliminate the observer. His behaviour to some extent was heroic and exemplary; to another extent, inappropriate. Before the awesome experience of death, the scientist needs to defer to some other aspect of self. The monk sought to make death into a heroic venture: not something the soul, or the foetus in the infant, suffers. The monk did not allow for the impiety of viewing one's own death as an area for experiment. He viewed life as an agnostic might view some imaginary descent into the underworld – as an episode which leaves the spirit dry (Evans-Wentz, 1949).

In writing my autobiography or in living out my life, I am faced by two unavoidable facts: one being my coming into the world, which I have forgotten, the other being my departure from it, which I cannot know. The incompleteness of the narrative is the source of its life. If I were able to imagine it as complete – as the Book of Judgement presumably is, or as 'definitive' biographies claim to be – it at once dies. The Book of Judgement, the 'definitive' biography, are dead in the way that salacious literature is dead: they are dehumanized. All true life stories can be couched in the terms of a dialogue between you and me. The gaps in the narrative, the unknowings, the absence of a third person, or biographer, are the source of life.

Notes

1 The neurotic wishes to fudge the issue that within him he has the culture of the killer and the torturer in an undefused state – and that, under certain slight changes in circumstance, this culture could explode. He has reason to be worried by the proximity of his neurotic world-view to psychotic disintegration. The trouble is he is too frightened of himself to be able to worry about this proximity. He worries, but his worries are displaced on to a self-idealizing concern with 'evaluation'. He prides himself on having a puritan conscience, the pride being the important thing.

2 W. R. Bion thought that to be able creatively to use the psychotic element in oneself was an indication of genius. Plato had this genius to an exceptional degree. The Platonic enquirer asserts that what is not there is the truth. The more it is not there the more it is the truth. Some means for registering that which is not there is required – the soul – and the fact that the soul is not there, either, is a triumphant demonstration of its importance. This book is an attempt to write about the soul, or the foetus that persists in the infant, the infinitely tender being that forever fluctuates between life and death and must endure God's contract, the creative act of being born: endurance which my everyday self seeks investments and divestments to deny.

3 I have taken this idea from the New Penguin Shakespeare edition of *The Tempest* (1968, p. 148): 'A blue colour in the eye-lid was regarded as a sign of pregnancy.'

3

The birth of Adam

There is another ego, according to whose
action the individual is unrecognisable, and
passes through, as it were, allotropic states
... [to discover] the same single radically
unchanged element. (... Diamond and coal
are the same pure single element of carbon.
The ordinary novel would trace the history of
the diamond – but I say: 'Diamond, what!
This is carbon.' And my diamond might be
coal or soot, and my theme is carbon.)
D. H. Lawrence to Edward Garnett,
5 June 1914

ADAM OPENS his eyes in paradise. The first
moment of human perception – no eye has
looked on a world before. What did Adam see? Adam knew
no past; his eyes were empty of the past. His eyes sought light
by looking into other eyes. If he is aware of mind (I
conjecture), it is of an anima outside him, flooding, pouring
in, through his eyes.

The priestly version of the Genesis Creation story (Genesis
1:2, 1–4) has him open his eyes on a world so complete that
he probably felt excluded by it. He had nothing to compare it
with.

He might have been an adult without a past, without
memory, all sound and sight without sense. No experience,
whether conscious or unconscious, of having been a foetus,
or born, or nurtured through infancy. He might have been

someone sent back from the dead, perceiving too much of everything: trees, camels, sun, darkness, lambs, plants, sky, sea, elephants, whales. A dead man flooded by experience – yearning to retreat into the promenades of the underworld.

Adam's first sight, on opening his eyes, would have been of a sublime mouth, within inches of his face, breathing life into his nostrils. God, kneeling over Adam, breathes life into him. The soul is someone else's breath, in Plotinus's terms, an emanation (and no more) of the Intelligible.

Soul is not like the reasonable, sensible self. It is as yielding as wax. God makes Adam in his own image: Adam is a God-fetish, a thing suffused with extraordinary power. The making, the utter yielding to the impression, is all. The Intelligible – unknowable powerful ideas – impress the soul in their likeness. The Deluge nearly drowns Noah, the storm nearly destroys Lear: deluges and storms of the mind. The soul fluctuates, ceases to exist, or (often reluctantly) flickers back to life.

Adam's dependence on the idea known as God for his existence does not allow him the belief that he has a separate mind. Theories of mind do not apply to him. Mind cherishes continuities: it needs families, societies, nations. It feeds on events in space and time. Soul – Adam as soul – has none of this. It exists only in its dependence on God, as one continuous breathing from the mouth of God.

When I enter a cathedral, such as the one at Ely, I do not ask: who made this place? I am not concerned with artistic personality or the placing of artistic personality in history. Nor do I find myself asking: who am I?

The gods of the place

This is our first night in a house in Dorset. It lives up to expectations. I awake just after midnight. Thunder. Barley-corn pillars of lightning rise from a distant sea.

A child sits before a piece of paper, takes pencil in hand and without hesitation releases an image on the page. There is no object before her. She does not transcribe: she gives no sign of transmitting some image from within. No frowning, no looking inward, no dreamy look in her eyes. Her pencil flows spontaneously; and yet her joy in her calligraphy, her knack – the way she catches the likeness of flower or balloon – is essentially human.

She marries pencil to paper and the drawing just appears. She feels no hunger for food; almost nothing can stop the pencil and paper from living out their existence together; their coming together creates a setting; and the setting is her inspiration.

When people tell us stories we usually want to know where they come from. I want to believe that there is something going on inside her which issues forth in images – I want to apply some model of inside and outside the self. The model fails to apply. Apparently the story has no history. It requires a concept of absolute creation *ex nihilo*, finding one model in the Genesis fiat perhaps. As in dreams, no source in authorship is traceable, except by inference, through the circumstance of the images.

Revelation

The other day it occurred to me that when I was young, thirty years ago, I used to believe that experience was revelation. Not how I see it now; and yet, suddenly, the idea brought back a past to which I had long felt indifferent – I vividly felt myself to be as I once had been, young, in the early 1950s, walking by a river one morning. In nearly every glance, a discovery: delight in the fortuitous conjunction of branches from two trees, the lap of water by the river's edge, rime on the grass. Nature was revelatory. I thought of these moments as epiphanies – using the term James Joyce had used to describe moments of heightened perception. Gods of the place! I did not realize that epiphany in its primary sense meant the appearance of a baby – a hallowed baby, infant before the Magi.

I was not looking for the uplift of a birth. Nor did I think of myself as looking for evidence of some primal and continuous creativity, the God who makes the world anew at every moment. My walk was a truancy. The random conjunctions of nature provided me with an alternative to the received opinions and celibacies of a culture which was too much like a priesthood. Existing for its own sake was important: I needed nothing else. To have a life meant to have consciousness; every moment was to be savoured; every moment was like a work of art; nothing was to be wasted.

Moments of delight were arrested by moments of despondency. Nothing delighted; nothing added up. I had a model for these shifts in feeling. In Italy, during early adolescence, I had taken lessons in Dante. 'Nel mezzo del cammin di nostra vita . . . ' Half-way down life's pathway was half-way to the grave, perhaps. I took it for granted that people had mid-life crises; mine, at seventeen, happened every few weeks.

Dante got out of his by finding himself guides – Virgil, then Beatrice – to take him into worlds figuratively unlike the natural one. He was not lost in some actual wood. Nor had he entered some actual hell as a consequence of being lost in some wood. Places had to be imagined to articulate his feelings.

Psychotic metaphysics

The writers of Genesis differ from Dante. They were convinced that God manifested himself in certain clear demarcated places. Genesis is non-allegorical. The God of Genesis exists here and not there, and the places he sanctifies are quite different from the places of allegory: they are actual; they do not refer to something outside themselves. The psychotic self recognizes this insight; the neurotic self has trouble with it. The Promised Land is not a metaphorically desirable place, a symbol for states of mind or futurity, as in the allegorical interpretation of it in the Epistle to the Hebrews; it is actual, the only place where God is; without it, we are done for. 'The spots where intercourse between heaven and earth took place were not willingly regarded as arbitrarily chosen but, on the contrary, were considered as having been somehow selected by the Deity Himself for His service' (Wellhausen, 1885, p. 30).

I need a psychotic metaphysic to understand this literalism: a theory of the fetish perhaps.

Imagine the universe to be made of thoughts, of ideas – ideas as powers, not concepts; and powers that assemble as energies and divisions. By divine decree, some of the powers become bodies, opaque in terms of their own substances, yet translucent with divinity and ancestral evocation. (The Australian aborigine calls such ancestral power in natural things, Dreamings.)

In his study of the Mycenean Tree and Pillar Cult, Sir Arthur Evans (1901) who led the excavations at Knossos, has described in detail the profound iconographic relationship between the Semitic and Mycenean cultures; and it would be fair to suppose with him that when Jacob lays down his head on a stone – in a place in the middle of nowhere that will soon be known as Bethel – that the stone has some kinship in its power to the Greek *baetylos*, or god-meteor that falls from the heavens. (In Greek mythology Baetylos is a son of the sky-god, Ouranos.)

Jacob leans his head against the stone, and the stone leaks the godhead into him – in the form of two dreams. It would seem that the intangible and unseeable ideas, having condensed into being an object of the senses – stone – now thin out, acquiring the translucence of dream-thoughts, as though returning to their former condition of being objects unavailable to the senses. In the first dream, the stone is transformed into an angelic ladder that transports divine beings between earth and heaven. In the second dream, God himself promises the dreamer the power of generation.

I suspect that Jacob's stone has a darker meaning, since his ability to dream is surely identifiable with the birthright, or right to generation, stolen from Esau; and the stone is one on which infants are slaughtered in sacrifice. Sir Arthur Evans discovered such a slaughter-stone in Macedonia a hundred years ago. 'Here beneath the same roof as the stone ... we were bidden to pass the night, so that the occult influences due to its spiritual possession might shape our dreams as in the days of the patriarchs' (Evans, 1901, p. 106).

In Freudian terms, I take the stone-fetish to provide a form of phallic osmosis (of both good and bad phallus) – knowledge by seepage, similar to Abraham's manner of sealing an oath with his eldest servant by having him put a hand on the patriarchal penis. 'Put, I pray thee, thy hand under my thigh' (Genesis 24:2). This is the theme of God's contract given a human demonstration in terms of male sexuality. That which can create is also that which (in phantasy at least) can destroy.[1]

Neurotic metaphysics

Neurotic metaphysics are more circumspect. The neurotic, while idealizing actual places (usually ones he has inhabited) never knows where he is. Present life has no clear meaning – and the neurotic has a commitment to feeling confused. Dante expects Virgil to help him discover meaning. The soul, face to face with experience, uncomprehendingly withdraws and imagines other structures. It may turn to allegory. The categories of human experience are heaven, hell and purgatory: idealized categories, not knowable actualities, however pleasant or unpleasant life might be.

In my view, states of confusion deserve a more interesting metaphor than the one of getting lost in woods; the bosky metaphor distracts the reader from the interesting element in the experience, the self observing its state of confusion and perhaps realizing that states of confusion are not necessarily stages in an allegorical journey. Dante leaps into figuration (and yet, on second thoughts, why not?); he does not explore the nature of the leap, or give the reason why he should wish it to occur. Getting metaphorically lost is transfigured into a motive for redemption. (This is very different from Cézanne's voluntary loss of control in seeking the 'motif'.)

I wonder whether I used once to approach epiphanies in

the same way — as motives for redemption. I did not think
that something actual was happening outside my mind, to
which mind was accidental. The Romantic interest, and
belief, lay in the overestimated importance ascribed to the
conjunction of mind and nature.

The meaningful appears and disappears, inviting the questing neurotic soul to describe it in terms of a journey through
metaphoric places. T. S. Eliot, in his *Four Quartets*, also
feared to get lost:

> ... not only in the middle of the way
> But all the way, in a dark wood, in a bramble,
> On the edge of a grimpen.

Puritans see value in the individual, unique properties of
experience. If it happens to them it must be important. They
mourn the loss of consciousness that will occur when they
die: so much investment in learning and polished introspection to be relinquished. If their experiences lose meaning,
they feel they are missing out on life. They reach out for
meaning through further metaphor:

> We had the experience but missed the meaning,
> And approach to the meaning restores the experience.
> *(Four Quartets)*

Milton's Adam — but not the Adam of Genesis — would have
found this view congenial. Meanings are preformationist,
carried seminally from generation to generation, through
anecdote and sacrament, as conductive as original sin:

> ... the past experience revived in the meaning
> Is not the experience of one life only
> But of many generations — not forgetting
> Something that is probably quite ineffable.
> *(Four Quartets)*

To meditate on the meaning of experience encourages the self
to identify with both the Adam within and the Adam in
history. At some metaphoric or incarnatory level, they are the

same. In Adam I die, in Christ I live. But metaphoric thinking of this kind, though pleasing, gets in the way of more important literal, psychotic truths.

Note

1 The impulse that discovers the sacred in specific places, in cults and particular containments, is similar in its kind of thinking to Aristotle's conception in his *Physics* of place as the adjacent boundary of the containing body – a theory which reputedly had an obstructive effect on the development of modern physics. Galileo's achievement in re-conceiving space as Euclidean (that is, as non-naturalistic space) and in realizing that the movement of bodies cannot be quantified in relation to some fixed point deserves to be held in creative assessment against other important trends in seventeenth-century thought: not least, the need to consider life in terms of allegorical places. My thinking in this regard has been helped by Max Jammer's (1954) *Concepts of Space* and Alexandre Koyré's writings on Galileo (Koyré, 1968, especially ch. 1).

4

Between life and death

*He looked at things with the eyes, so it
seemed, of a man who had been at the brink
of death and to whom, as he emerges from the
darkness, the world reveals itself as un-
fathomably beautiful and mysterious . . . Existence was one continuous convalescence; it
was as though he were newly re-born from a
mortal illness every day of his life.*

Aldous Huxley,
Introduction to D. H. Lawrence. Letters

ALDOUS HUXLEY was close to being blind
himself. Lawrence had intuitions of an other-
worldly kind – puckish, supernatural, a bit uncanny. He saw
things, Huxley thought, with 'convalescent eyes'. The journey through illness ferried him through tributaries of an
underworld river.

Huxley does not say what the convalescent eyes might have
seen during times of illness. A blurring of vision, the emergence of ghost-like shapes perhaps, the deliria of a high
temperature. Loss of sight, Huxley implies, is comparable to
being dead. It is not absence of sight, blankness – if you want
to understand being blind, someone once claimed, try to
imagine an eye in the back of your skull, seeing what at
present you cannot see. Lawrentian loss of sight is a visual
sensation of darkness, an earthy tangible darkness.

In dyings of this kind, you enter a positive condition of
darkness, a state of dreaming without visual images: a state
of mental generation in which there is nothing to hold on to

in thought or sensation. The self asleep lies close to the pulse of creativity – close to Persephone and Pluto, queen and king of the underworld, in a realm beyond the realms of sight.

When Huxley describes Lawrence as being 'newly re-born from mortal illness every day of his life', he describes an exceptional way of emerging from the condition of a non-visual sleep-thought. Certain states of sleep, like certain states of illness, modify perception. Recovering from sleep, waking up from illness, even (figuratively) returning from the dead, is the precondition for a certain kind of perception. A dream dreams us and, in so doing, organizes our conscious percep-tions. Astonishment in genius explodes from some structural fault or shift in dream – movement from one state of being to another, a death, a rebirth.

Admittedly, the eyes of the dead are sightless; and most of us have enjoyed the game of closing our eyes and imagining ourselves as dead; otherwise, death and blindness have no persuasive similarity.

Coming back to life, if we can imagine this process – as disagreeable, probably, as a thawing out – is limited to the experience of seeing once more. On this point, Lawrence is a Platonist. He would have agreed with Huxley. Or Milton. Insight is acquired through the loss of actual sight. Convales-cent eyes are eyes that temporarily are sightless – the self pulsing in the blood-flow of the primal couple, the under-world coupling of the royal lovers in death, Pluto and Persephone.

In the poem, 'Bavarian Gentians', Lawrence looks into the blueness of the Bavarian gentian and finds himself guided down darker and darker stairs – 'here blue is darkened on blue.' Here Persephone goes, 'to the sightless realm where darkness is awake upon the dark,' where the lovers are, 'among the splendours of torches of darkness, shedding darkness on the lost bride and groom.'

To be one of the Lawrentian dead is to be the foetus in the womb, sentient without sight, held in close by its mother, in mysterious sympathy, as her lover pulses life through her.

Perhaps the foetus senses that this life-flow is the source of its own coming into being. (And perhaps states of non-being in later life – impotent incarnations, the self as revenant – indicate estrangements from foetal sympathies.)

A foetus will flinch if a torch is shone on its mother's abdomen. Moving within its moving mother, it is probably aware of changes in light density on the uterine skin-screen – as when at night its mother returns to the shades of her bed.

I remember a Lawrence story I had read years ago as being about a dead man who returns to his wife from the battle-fields of the First World War. I was confusing two stories: one of which, 'The Man who Returns from the Dead', is a story about the experiences of Jesus in the cave, as he returns to life; the other, 'The Blind Man', being about a man who returns without sight from the war.

In the darkness of the stables, Maurice is sure in tending to the horses. His wife Isabel close to him, unable to communicate with him, feels frightened by her inability to see in darkness. Later, upstairs in the house Maurice

> ... seemed to know the presence of objects before he touched them ... So long as he kept this sheer immediacy of blood-contact with the substantial world he was happy, he wanted no intervention of visual consciousness. In this state there was a certain rich positivity, bordering some-times on rapture. Life seemed to move in him like a tide lapping, lapping, and advancing, enveloping all things darkly. (Lawrence, 1934, p. 251)

His effect on Isabel's friend, Bertie, is like the presence of death itself. He runs his fingers over Bertie's horrified face and impels him, like some doubting, recoiling Thomas, to touch blind eyes and scarred face. It is too much for Bertie: 'He was like a mollusc whose shell is broken' (p. 259).[1]

Lawrence sees the ship which carries him into death as Noah's Ark. He does not see the Ark as the one point of life in a death world, as the one surviving element in the flood of oblivion. He sees it as invaded by the death experience, the epitome of the death experience; in some way, perhaps, engendering the death of the world.

Huxley thinks that Lawrence's convalescent eyes were his from birth: his sensibility had been formed by the repetition of lifelong states of eclipse. And he had been broken by the war. Like Noah, Lawrence knew a chronic condition of mental dying which those who actually drown probably have no awareness of. The emotional drowning of Noah – the unknowing of the Noah as knower – entails an imaginative experience of obliteration. There is a coldness more cold than any cold in temperature, and dyings worse than any death. Gilgamesh, looking out of the portholes of the Ark, is tear-drowned at the sight of a non-existent world, a bleak dawn waste of water and sky. Compare Lawrence's 'The Ship of Death':

> There is no port, there is nowhere to go
> only the deepening blackness darkening still
> blackness upon the soundless, ungurgling flood . . .

The traveller mistakenly thinks to enter oblivion. Dawn returns – cruelly he thinks – and oblivion and the state of illness recede. In some way, he returns to life.

> The flood subsides, and the body, like a worn sea-shell
>   emerges strange and lovely,
> And the little ship wings home.

Trust not the teller, trust the tale, thought Lawrence. Tellers perish, or they tell lies: they are untrustworthy. The mythic imagination does not concern itself with obliteration or questions of untruth. Tales persist, unchanging, outside time, although they may be about change and breakdown.

The Ark carries a sample of the earth's ecology through states of destruction into the new world. The universe survives, narrowly. Look, we have come through! affirms Lawrence. His body travels close to death repeatedly, until at last it crosses the frontier. He was aware of the body's journey into the psychic underworld. And he was matter-of-

fact about it: this is how things are. You come close to death
– you enter the underworld and somehow, on one occasion at
least, you do not return.

Actual breakdown occurs in the Tower of Babel story – so
profound a breakdown that the Genesis narrative breaks off.
It is as though the book of Genesis could not be continued.
Inconsequentially, the narrative picks up once more with the
story of Abraham and Sarah: the travails of a couple who are
unable to have a baby. The issue is only incidentally a
biological one. Finding its bearings once more, Genesis
returns to its theme: God's making of a covenant with man
(the figure of Abraham having replaced Adam). The nature of
the covenant is not directly bound to questions of fertility and
transmission. But they are necessarily bound to it.

Absolute creativity

To seal the contract, the visionary architect himself sets his
bow in the cloud. Like a bridge, the rainbow vaults across the
sky, joining one rim of the earth to another. A brilliant
spectrum gathers the horizons together, leaps up, crosses
space and curves downwards, beautiful in its strength. But it
is made of raindrops. Its promise is uncertain; and it will
evaporate.

The contract insists on the existence of an absolute creativity – one that exists beyond the scope of mind, in some way
inimical to the actions of mind. Or so the rainbow tells me. If
I acknowledge the existence of absolute creativity, it in turn
will underwrite the quality of my existence. It will grant me a
right that I may never be conscious of – to be the vehicle for
certain processes of life and death. This right is not a Faustian
inheritance: it in no way satisfies my conscious appetites.

The convenant guarantees that life will move through me
in ways that I cannot understand; life will fluctuate, weaken
or intensify in ways that I can seldom perceive; and have me
undergo a fate whose seriousness I might sometimes wish to
disavow. I am considering legalities and illegalities that do
not necessarily lead to sophisticated theories about natural

law. Legality and illegality appear to be primordial issues in any form of contract, as in the moment when I allow myself to look at the sky.

Perfection

I look at the sky. What I see seems perfect to me: the sky presents me with a perfection which I cannot add to or subtract from without spoiling it. I am like Adam – it is as though I had opened my eyes for the first time. I am overwhelmed by the completeness of the experience. The sky possesses my consciousness in some way that overrides the notion of consciousness. Questions of intonation, or personal timbre, or the flavour of minds exchanging information with each other have no bearing on my perception. The sky indicates another realm: one unavailable to thought.

I cannot meddle with what I now see and I cannot deny it. The sky is undeniable. It is beyond the powers of my imagination to have imagined the sky that I perceive. My imagination has met more than its match; it feels over-whelmed. Or rather imagination, as an element of personality, feels disbarred.

I try to think of the sky as a work of art: that is, as something made by an artist. It occurs to me that all human works of art would be rendered superfluous when compared to the sky as a work of art. They lack its authority. Its perfection heightens my sense of the imperfection of any object a human being might make. When I lie in bed and sink into sleep, an image of the sky comes to mind, the sky at dawn, palely red, with fading stars. The image bears in on me. It is not transposable or changeable, as many images are.

The more undeniable I find the sky, the more uncertain do I find my own existence to be. Its perfection calls in doubt the nature of my imperfect existence. To some extent, this threat to the certitudes of well-being happens all the time. All experience tells me: you could not have made me up. I am beyond your means of imagining or conceiving. Before me you have to admit inadequacy. There is an anti-symbolizing quality in all experience. Experience challenges me to undergo it as though I did not have a mind that thinks, that observes conventions, that transposes. The anti-symbolic exists in the here-and-now; it insists on some literal mind-denying response.

There are experiences where it is the experience that matters, not who has the experience or who transmits it or who responds to it. There are unknown experiences which are unconscious. There may be unknown experiences which have no relationship to conscious or unconscious thoughts and that exist in some realm beyond human discrimination.

The unknown God is able to think with each element of the universe, however primitive the element. All things are elements in his thought, all things are mind – potentially thoughts which the God-mind can hold in communication with itself. Or conversely, all thoughts are things, God being on the side of naïve realism, some system which dissolves mind and the symbolic activities which make up thought. God may be some anti-symbolic tendency inimical to the interpretative impulse of mankind.

Adam and Abraham would have found intuitions of this kind familiar. The vegetative and animal levels of awareness that Aristotle ascribed to the foetus are modes that the modern mind does not recognize. There may also be anti-symbolic states of intuition, which mankind has largely mislaid. Dogs often know when they are going to die; unlike many human beings who live in a dissociated state from the foetal compass of life and death intuitions within them.

Unknowable experiences exist for which we have no responsibility – natural dying being among them. Or miscarriages. Or other tragic accidents. When I was ill, the amazing thought occurred to me that possibly I was not responsible for my illness. It was something that had happened to me. The 'it' was unknown. Was the 'it' an 'it' that I could never know?

Battlefield

Huxley believed that Lawrence's convalescent eyes saw the world with an unusual wonder. Convalescent eyes are eyes that tremulously continue to reflect the helplessness and blurring of illness; they see the underworld translucence in an overworld object: they peer for evidences of life. It need not be this way. The unsealing of eyes, and the return from death, might be disenchanting.

The way in which I view the world when I return from the dead depends to some extent on how I experienced the state of being that occurs between life and death, as I sense it in illness, or in dreams, or on the battlefield. The reality of the world may make me feel unreal. But the reality of the other-world – of illness, of the battlefield, of covenant-making with an unknowable God – may diminish the seeming reality of the actual world. Possibly Noah was unable to believe in the post-deluvial world and thought of it as some distant and unpleasant dream. Possibly he moved through it in so guilt-ridden a fashion that he felt himself to be a sleepwalker. An isolated individual, contemplating the destruction of a generation, may be unable to find release from the condition of grieving.

Many find the world unreal when they return from the battlefield. At times I doubt whether I am alive. I want to bring myself alive. Some people stick knives into themselves, or use their bodies violently to demonstrate to themselves that they are actually alive. Conceivably, some people might commit suicide to convince themselves that they had been alive. Cartesian doubt includes the psychological state of doubting the extent to which my moment-to-moment existence is meaningful. The possible deception of the senses is related to a possible numbness of the senses, as in depression. In depression nothing can seem real; everything is dispossessed. Is this some form of truth?

Noah knew that most living things had been destroyed. I conjecture that, as an aspect of the unfolding of his humanity, Adam in Eden would have wondered guiltily where his non-existent parents and their other children had gone.

Doggy

A woman who behaved in ways that indicated that she thought – unconsciously at least – that she was a ghost, had a dream in which there were two blood-stained indentations on a wall: probably tooth marks. She said her puppy persisted in biting and chewing everything up. On Sunday she had taken the puppy for a walk – by a pond. It had fallen into the pond and she had felt disabled and unable to help it as it sank. She had feared it would drown. It had not drowned. It had risen to the surface of the water and doggy-paddled to dry land.

She had recently become pregnant; and from her previous history, she had some reason to believe that she might miscarry. She had left the dog to its own devices as a kind of testing: as a form of allowing it to die and to be reborn, an act of baptism, a proving that existing beings require the categories of life and death in order to be alive; more cruelly, as a pseudo-scientific form of experiment, like witch-ducking. She thought much of Jesus and the Crucifixion: a belief that the good and innocent are inevitably sacrificed lay at the core of her pessimism.

More than once in the waiting-room, she had found herself contemplating an image in her mind of a calm and attractive lake. Her associations made it clear that she imagined myself and my family as drowned at the bottom of the lake. She felt left out from our life, so she wished us dead. She feared to come alive herself because she feared a biting dog-infant in herself. She dreaded, and often found hard to control, an impulse to be cruel to children whom she cared about. She tended to project violent infant impulses into her actual children; and she claimed that their naughtiness left her disabled, as the submerged dog had done.

Note

1   It becomes like a madness at last, to know that one is all the time walking in a pale assembly of an unreal world – this house, the furniture, the sky and the earth – whilst oneself is all the while a piece of darkness pulsating in shocks, and the shocks and the darkness are real . . . Keep somewhere, in the darkness of reality, a connection with me. I feel there is something to go through – something very important. It may be it is only in my soul – but it seems to grow more and more looming, and this day time reality becomes more and more unreal, as if one wrote from a grave – or womb – they are the same thing, at opposite extremes. (Letter to Bertrand Russell, March 1915, in Moore, 1962, p. 330)

5

Tales without tellers

HELL, HEAVEN and other imaginable places are categories of an autobiographical kind – ways of dealing with states of confusion and not knowing. I do not understand my experience: I put it into categories which may make some sense of it. In the Genesis story, the categories are not given: no hell, no heaven, and no Satan either, or Adam's dream, as in Milton.

The reader of Genesis may bring self-awareness to the story; but the issue of self-awareness does not exist in the narrative itself. A priest, following Genesis, would want to describe his rites as impersonal, tales without teller, irrefutable in ways that objects in consciousness are not. It matters little if no one attends his church, or if he should die and be replaced by another priest. The act of primal creation, and the idea of the covenant which inevitably derives from the act of creation, exist outside consciousness. The priest in his rites relives the act of primal creation automatically, in a manner only marginally related to consciousness.

Genesis enacts a condition that is not selfhood. It does not – perhaps cannot – describe the condition. It enacts a condition that forfeits any notion of the personal or the individual. In thoughts about our own dying, or in dreams, we have hints of this condition: mythic experiences, encounters in which the self and the other exist on a level before self-definition has come into being. I do not learn what God or Adam are thinking; thinking, in the sense that I understand it, is not what they are concerned with.

The focus is on story. Stories are told again and again. The story, in essence, does not change. To quote from Robert Graves's poem, 'To Juan at the Winter Solstice', 'There is one story and one story only . . . ' Gathering everything into one story is a monist's ideal; it is made possible by having a massive unknowability at the centre of the story, into which all variation can be reconciled. The one-story interpretation of things is like a wheel in which all the spokes lead to the same (unknowable) axle.

To this extent, story-tellers and listeners exercise no influence over their tales. The story is eternal recurrence, inspiration from the same source taking different forms. A succession of patriarchs (who are always Everyman) enter into transactions with an idea so powerful that no one can be sure whether it is creative or destructive. The idea makes, moulds, buffets the patriarchs beyond belief. Lives are determined by unknown ideas. The engagement with an absolute and unknowable idea – intolerable goodness! – exists on a level on which individuality has no meaning.

The idea – the absolute creation of God's first act – is not a fiction. It does not resemble fiction. The human ability to create fictions has a certain authority. When compared to the power of absolute creation, the authority is eclipsed: fiction-making turns out to be a luxurious superfluity.

Absolute creation exists in a dimension in which qualities of mind or flavours of consciousness are irrelevant. Pre-personal, it enters into transactions in which all men are undifferentiated. It undermines the bases on which all fiction rests: it sees consciousness as a kind of fiction.

In the modern view, stories necessarily exist in the mind of the characters sometimes, in the mind of the narrator always. Stories tend to be autobiographical, revealing of the mind of the author, often in ways that the author might not wish. The Genesis story does not follow this procedure. It is not like *Paradise Lost*, which clearly reflects the personality of both Milton and Adam.

Does the whole thing occur in God's consciousness? There is no evidence to suggest that God creates a fictional narrative of himself in the act of absolute creation. The creator of an absolute creation disdains fiction-making. He may even think of it as a profanity. The Tower of Babel, which rises like a shaft of light falling, is an object as wrought as a story; and it marks profanity on an actual spot of ground. It transacts profanely between heaven and earth and must be destroyed: it is a fiction, a literary babble, a translators's conference, rather than a creation.

Thinking of the Babel kind – exercising consciousness, constructing hypotheses – is not God-like. God, like Newton, claims not to feign hypotheses. God, like Newton (and Newton's apologist, Locke) posits an absolute creation and a blankness in the receptor's mind.

God acts. Absolute creation has no limits. God's token judgements on the creation, his finding it good, is a way to pace out the rhythm of the Creation. God is the Creation in some spontaneous, pre-conscious and impersonal form. From a non-anthropocentric view, God's act of creation is mystery; and mystery cannot be projected into. God is not Adam's puppet; nor is Adam puppet to God. One issues into the other's breath: their lungs are at one in the act of breathing.

The Genesis Creation is without human awareness, devoid of human intentions and beliefs in responsibility. Adam is quiescent – until the moment when he is invited to name the animals. Adam shows no sign of thinking. It would be misleading to think that he must have projected his mind into the universe.

Global projection

Consider the case of someone in therapy who projected aspects of his mind to an almost global extent. He talked about the world as though he did not exist in it. He described a world that was garbled in meaning, listless and empty. The people who inhabited the world tended to conspire against him – in a desultory fashion. It was very hard to tune into him. If I listened carefully, I did have the sensation that on the rim of his world there existed a predatory waiting intelligence, shadowy and controlling, faintly colouring every empty event. He presented emptiness with calculation, intending to deceive and disappoint. He accepted the view that he was passive – was self-congratulatory about it, and mildly enjoyed the thought that he was controlled by a presence that intended to disappoint and deceive.

He was not like a revenant from the dead or a man driven into phantom states by the harshness of the world. He behaved as though he were stopping someone else from being born, a baby responsive to nurture. He was committed to spite – being spiteful was his way of grasping on to the idea of potency. He once dreamt of a fine London plane tree outside my work-room 'with its balls and seeds', and then of a car so flooded that its owner could not get it started. He acknowledged the existence of a potent father in the tree, while in effect urinating into his mother so that she should be disabled. He did not exercise his murderous rivalry to his father directly – out of fear perhaps; out of a taste for slyness certainly.

A part of me has to be born to be able to be so controlling or to be so given over to projection. The self before birth does not think to have an environment to project into – since it has reason to believe that its environment is an enfolding extension of self, not an otherness. If projections occur, they must occur within the self, into some fabricated otherness within the self.

Creation and fiction

Let us assume that Adam, in a dissociated way, is the author of the story. He is alone. He imagines God and the Creation of the universe and he projects his imagining into space. God would be Adam's hallucination. It is not Adam who is being breathed into by God; it is Adam who makes God through his breathing. The ventriloquist's doll creates the ventriloquist. Imagine God, Eve and the serpent to be projected elements of Adam himself.

To follow this reading would be to claim that the Creation was a form of fiction-making. But by its nature, the act of creation has a reality which fiction cannot encompass. It exists in some form that precedes the existence of fiction; as on the psychotic level of mind, which can experience creation but cannot conceive of fiction.

The Adam of Genesis is not Milton's Adam, who has thoughts, talks to parental figures, has dreams and behaves with the scruples of a Puritan. Genesis does not allow the human figure freedom of interpretation. It describes a psychological dimension in which freedom of interpretation does not exist. Human fiction-making and conjecture disappear in the face of a primal creation. I would wish to avoid this level, as I would wish to avoid psychotic elements in myself, for fear of being destroyed.

Adam does not disable thought; he is pre-thought. The world is too much for him. He has no space; he is an extension of the God-substance, the breath in God's lungs. He is in no position to ask: how did the world come about? He is unable to have thoughts. But he is not dehumanized or brainwashed.

Compare him to someone who believes that the world consists of nothing but his thoughts – that every time he has a different conception of God; a different God would come into being. The unknowable otherness is populated by attempts to define it – Genesis implies this possibility. The writers of the Priestly text and the writers of the Yawistic text have different conceptions of God; and these two Gods exist

41

side by side. Being pre-individualistic, there is no conflict in their having the same name.

All men are Adam in the Adamic transaction with the unknowable idea of primal creation. Noah, Abraham and other patriarchs relive the same story; and, generation by generation, mankind continues the reliving.

I would associate the kind of thinking in Genesis with transmigration or reincarnation myths which transcend questions of individual consciousness – being like D. H. Lawrence's conception of the psyche as it exists before the development of an individual awareness. Theories of transmigration and reincarnation apply to conditions that have beings, in terms of development, before the emergence of theories of attention: one mind being aware that another mind is focusing it, or has disappeared, or has returned.

Tardema

Opening his eyes, what did Adam see? Did he sense futurity, the entire race within him – had he, even then, acquired testicles? Will I discover the meaning of the first image in his eyes as the last image fades in mine?

God puts Adam to sleep; creates Eve; would seem to make Eve out of Adam's body while Adam is asleep. Adam plays no active part in God's parturition. His sleep is possibly a void; all mind is in God; and all God-mind exists as absolute creativity; it cannot be questioned or modified or worked on.

God's creativity does not have the pliancy of human thought; it does not raise hypotheses. God makes Eve in order to complete a pattern. The animal kingdom consists of couples – and God gives Adam a mate to complete the symmetry. The patternings of nature indicate a creativity very different from the hesitant makings of fiction.

In Hebrew (I learn) the word for Adam's sleep – *tardema* – describes Abraham's sleep in Genesis 15. Adam names the animals and then sinks into a sleep, whose contents in consciousness, if any, are unrecorded. Abraham sacrifices certain animals and then enters sleep in a fear of darkness.

God blesses his futurity. Does Abraham dream God, or does the God beside him communicate through dormant senses?

The question is possibly unanswerable. To be able to link the naming of the animals and the making of Eve implies a theory of symbol-making that Genesis does not accommodate. In Genesis, Adam does not directly communicate with the reader; his consciousness is not given; nor is it seen to modify our perception of the events.

Adam has little power; he is like a newborn or a mentally damaged older child. There is no direct communication in consciousness between him and us. We sense a deeper bond – an unknowable binding to all creation. It is possible, with very damaged children, to intuit a continuing transaction with an unknown God: a more serious and worthwhile existence than any I might be usually accustomed to. (Yet it exists within me.)

A nine-year-old blind child in therapy appeared to be in conversation with somebody or something but without self-awareness or much ability to communicate with fellow human beings. He lived out a spiritual dialogue with the unknown, which did not have the dimension of the autobiographical. Was I deceived in thinking his behaviour revealed mental activity?

His experience of life, I infer, had been one of cruel deception. His projecting of the possibility of cruel deception into me was evidence of his having an active psychic life. My carrying any doubts he might have had about the probity of his object, the internal presence with whom he talked, perhaps strengthened his capacity to continue to communicate with it.

Adam does not doubt God: he has no psychic space in which to entertain doubt. He is faced by the evidence of an overwhelming, irrefutable and unceasing creation. Revelation assaults his senses, inducing incoherence. If he were to realize the possibility of doubt in himself, he would have nowhere to put it.

His doubt might have taken the form of a fear that he would be cruelly deceived. He has nowhere to put his fear into – until Eve appears. She is a possible receptacle for the fiction: 'I have been cheated.' In allowing him to exercise a capacity for doubt, she allows him to enter into the processes of development.

Autobiography begins when there is a situation which allows the thinker to exercise his doubt – doubt being a space between God and him, in which he can converse with himself about whether he can discover other forms of life from the one he shares with God. Will he discover the freedom within himself to deny God's superiority?

The Yawistic writers intuit Adam's helplessness and utter dependence on God. They understand the mythic atmosphere required if certain kinds of symbolization are to occur. The Priestly writers understand Adam differently: they consider him to be some kind of priest, or severely damaged infant, who subscribes to autistic rites, bound to a pathological notion of commitment which cannot contain the flavour of a personal consciousness, unable to dramatize doubt – doubt being something you project into the errant congregation and the unfaithful, the princes of Babylon and Egypt.

6

The buried source of light

I DO NOT think my father ever exorcized his guilt over having survived the battlefields of the First World War. Perhaps I am writing now hopefully to exorcize his guilt. He did not speak about the war if he could avoid it. The stories he told were often the stories that silence implies. I think that this country, and more than this country, is still sunk in depression because of that war.

In psychic reality, an object is disabled or lost, buried, forgotten. But not destroyed. It continues to exist somewhere, waiting to be rediscovered. It sets up intimations. It beams out energies. The dead continue to speak to the living. Sometimes they return like admonishing revenants, sometimes making a more savage impression. What is this object in psychic reality? Does it mark inspiration or death, creation or destruction? Its presence can be discovered everywhere, and especially in stories.

In the Syriac *Book of the Rolls*, a long-lost book, probably written by Clement the Apostle in the sixth century AD (Gibson, 1901), God makes Adam so literally in his image that Adam is more deity than man. He is not properly distinguished from the deity: he has not a separable mind. He is foetal – a personality in religious communion. Human experience, sluiced by divinity, has the property of dream; it radiates with a dream light. In Clement's account, Adam is no thing of clay or dust into which God breathes soul; or if he is, he has been transformed into a fetish of the most dangerous kind, since he is not aniconic. He is made in the image of God; and his sublimity frightens the angels.

> They were affrighted. The wondrous glory upon his face terrified them. His form appeared shining with divine light greater than the light of the sun . . . He drew himself up – he leapt standing. He was in the centre of the earth. He stretched out his right hand and his left hand and put his feet in order upon Golgotha. (Gibson, 1901, p. 6)

The earth becomes meaningful from the fact of Adam's being at its centre. His power radiates through the universe: he is God in man, God in body, God in all material things. His feet rest on Golgotha, the skull-hill. When he dies, he will be lodged there, under the skull-hill, until the end of time.

I want to think of this mode of thinking as delusional because I cannot relate it to my experience. It makes me feel helpless. Conceptualism, the use of language as a tool for understanding – Adam's naming of the animals – is one way of responding to experience and of managing the world. I need to manage the world. But the belief that God made Adam in his own image – or that he created Eve while mysteriously insisting that Adam should be asleep – indicates an entirely different field, and one which casts me into helplessness: a controversial field, in which physical happenings are believed to have the properties of thought, and in which the perceptions of waking life are indistinguishable from the imagery of dreams. To confuse the thing-ness of things with dream-images leads to an apocalyptic manner of description – revealing of the poetic nature of experience, or mad, we cannot be sure.

Spirit possesses body – spirit can possess any body. We cannot be sure whether the spirit is bad or good. In states of mourning the mourner, cast into doubt, wonders (as did Hamlet) whether the beloved voice of a dead father might be devil-possessed. Clement is perturbed by those who make images of the dead. They make images, he thinks, because they fear that they will lose their memories of the dead; they will be left with nothing; they must trade with unholy forces to summon up apparitions; they are seduced into acts of false memory. Clement is convinced that desperate attempts to remember the dead through images fill the world with sin. God destroys the world because of its idol-making – its attempts to simulate something that has been lost. In idol-making, in acts of representation, some seduction occurs; the act of mourning becomes a mine of wickedness.

A rich man died. His son, Clement informs us, made a golden image and placed it on the dead man's tomb. The devil, coming to possess the voice of the dead man, entered the golden image and invited the son to enter into a pact: if the son were to murder his own child in ritual sacrifice he would acquire all the arts of witchcraft. He would have unlimited wealth and power. Jacob's stone was aniconic, non-representational; the golden image made by the dead man's son was representational and therefore dangerous.[1]

Out of guilt, in grief, we may sacrifice everything that we love. But God must suffer this fate also. For God makes a representational image – in its first form, Adam; in its second form, Christ – and he must pay a heavy price for having done so. He makes Adam in his own image, as though Adam were the golden image on the tomb. Almost inevitably, the devil, in the form of a serpent, slides into Adam; and in turn God must enter into a pact with Adam in which he will, under the pressure of grief, offer up his son in sacrifice to redeem the world. Representation must result in sacrifice.[2]

Both Adam and Noah leave testaments for their successors. Their lives are lived out in their leaving of legacies. Every act of theirs has a future; is potentially recordable; is potentially an anecdote in the family bible or family history. The patriarch lives in a way intended to be known by the future – but dangerous when articulated. In sorrow we come to knowledge of what has always been known, but seldom thought about.

Both testators are concerned with the disposition of Adam's body after death. Adam asks Seth, his son, to have him buried in the Cave of Treasure; he hopes in time that his body will be taken to the centre of the earth. His wishes are delayed. The Deluge occurs. Noah takes Adam and the other dead patriarchs on board the Ark as the essential patrimony; they are as important to the future as seeds or the couplings of animals; they are like the stories essential to well-being and identity passed down by family and nation.

The body of Adam, as the spirit of God in man, a portent of Christ in a dark cave awaiting resurrection, converts the interior of the Ark into a shrine, a place of vigil, a cathedral within the waters; as on wintry mornings, the cathedral at Ely rides like an Ark over the waters of the Fens. The journey through drowning waters is the time of vigil. At the end of time, Clement thinks, life will be renewed.

In his testament, long after the Flood, Noah instructs Japheth to follow the guidance of the angel of God and secretly to take Adam's body to the centre of the earth. The story told by generation to generation will bring back the dead again, or if not the individual dead, will revive the family or nation, or the species. The stories are passwords. Adam pulses the energies of renewal from the centre of the earth: and the passing of time becomes deeply meaningful, as it does during the period of pregnancy; the passing of time is filled with expectation.

A monk keeps the Hours in vigil for the Second Coming. He marks the stages of his journey through consciousness to oblivion. In his testament, Adam recalls the time in paradise when every hour had its apportioned rituals of prayer and recollection, as much demarcated in time as is the recording of the daily acts of primal creation in Genesis; even the devils

48

have an hour when they are worshipped, an hour when they can do no harm. Family stories, prayer-like, mark out the interim as though on a clock-face, impersonally.

Grief holds on to the shreds of the beloved dead, a loveliness of mind which already has begun to disintegrate. Memories are unique. It is Adam, our first father, and not some unknown God who rests at the centre of the skull-hill as a living, unseen, all-powerful, forgotten memory. He is dead, inert; and yet he will remain charged with future power, pulsing, until the end of time. Meanwhile, the all-powerful primal creator, who re-makes the world at every moment, has – in the sublime act of his makings – become identified with extremes of ignobility and suffering. The Augustinian newborn, who suffers absolute pain in eternity, is God himself: insupportable mystery. At the time of the Deluge, millions sank beneath the water. Hands and hair streamed upwards. In my mind's eye, I cannot see the looks on their faces.

Primal creation includes primal suffering – it assumes all pain. After the Fall of Adam, Clement's God comes to him and sorrowfully says that for his sake he, the absolute God, the only artist, will become foetus, infant, child – suffer the world and submit to the nails of the Cross. He will live out the infancy Adam never had and, in dying, he will become the body in the skull-hill, the body of Adam. This is Clement's argument.

In family stories the dead for a while perambulate the world. In dreams, more vividly, they peer at us through misty windows. In revelation they come alive in other less mediated ways. Often they are objects of guilt. Not only those who survive the battlefield or the death camps may be tormented by memories of the dead. Noah, or Gilgamesh, look out from some aperture in the Ark into the wastes of sea. Do those who drown before them project an irredeemable madness into them and all the living?

49

Notes

1 An object, though buried, continues to beam with light. My miserable surroundings may yet contain an inspiration which owes nothing to space–time linearities. As Adam, I dream of an Eve whom God creates. She rises up before me out of the darkness, as though emerging from some earthly place of burial.

2 The serpent is chthonic, an earth-presence, a creature adored by the earth-mother from which it emerges. It is a threat to anyone outside the womb – especially to anyone who can claim no experience of having been a foetus. It is something from within – it has penile qualities to be sure, but primarily it lays claim on feeling as being the foetal existence that was denied to Adam: Abel in prototype to Adam's Cain.

> And truly I was afraid, I was most afraid,
> But even so, honoured still more
> That he should seek my hospitality
> From out the dark door of the secret earth.
>
> He drank enough
> And lifted his head, dreamily, as one who has drunken,
> And licked his tongue like forked night on the air, so
>   black,
> Seeming to lick his lips,
> And looked around like a god, unseeing, into the air . . .
>   (D. H. Lawrence, 'Snake', Taormina)

In *The Raw and the Cooked*, Claude Lévi-Strauss describes a beautiful Bororo myth which brings together all these possibilities, including the transformation of the Adam-foetus into the sacrificed Christ:

> A woman named Aturuaroddo picked up a piece of a boa that her husband had killed; the blood coming from the snake's flesh penetrated into her and fertilized her. While still in the womb, the 'son of the blood' conversed with his mother and suggested that he should help her to gather wild fruit. He emerged in the form of a snake, climbed a tree, picked the fruit, and threw it down for his mother to collect. She tried to run away from him, but he caught up with her and returned to the shelter of the womb.
>
> The woman was horrified and confided in her elder

brothers who organized an ambush. As soon as the snake emerged and climbed the tree, the mother ran away; when he came down to go after her, the brothers killed him. The body was burnt on a woodpile, and from the ashes sprouted the urucu bush, the resin tree, tobacco, maize and cotton. (Lévi-Strauss, 1964, p. 104)

7

Against the self

THE AUTOBIOGRAPHICAL impulse in Western culture (as I recognize it in myself) is often thought to originate with Augustine. It is a strange mixture of yearning and confession. The yearning, Platonist in kind, is for certitudes: and these certitudes, in an uncertain world, insist on being unworldly. The yearner comes to the view that sensations are deceiving and inimical to insight. Experience yields up meanings at best confusedly. Evidences of a reliable truth, both within and without the self, are dispersed, semi-concealed and even, on occasion, thought to be opposed to the interests of the self. An enemy to my sense of satisfaction goads me from within.

I find myself under pressure, internal pressure, to be penitent. I feel guilty, condemned without trial. I sense some presence that impels me into admitting my unworthiness and into having me examine my past life. The pressure encourages me to give it a personality in the form of an unkind object – in the case of Augustine, the presence of an exacting

God. Without the pressure, or the object, the need to think autobiographically would hardly occur. Without presences in the mind, felt to be bullying, or encouraging, or easily seducible perhaps, there would be no need to find a notation for my life. (I might write my autobiography in music or in painting as well as in words.) So far as I can see, there is nothing in the living of the present moment that impels me to think about the past or my peculiar involvement with past, present and future – unless that is, I perceive in the present moment foreshadowings of the inner presence.

The object makes me feel unworthy. I feel unworthy only in part through my falling into a category which the object and I mutually agree to be the sinful. Experience in itself, in so far as I can separate it from pressure, communicates a diffused sense of inadequacy. I find myself saying in regard to experience, 'Surely there is more to life than this,' while it, in turn, seems to say to me, 'I am important because I show you up as a defective witness; and you are defective as a witness in part because of the limitations in my manner of revealing.'

In asserting its importance, experience seems to admit to some defect in the range of its communication. It communicates untruly. For the Platonist, experience indicates intelligibilities which it cannot directly embody – how it does so is uncertain. Experience hints at something other than itself, some element alien to the experiential, which I cannot grasp because I think I can only come to understanding through experience.

Coleridge believed that a clue to this element had been given to him through his reading of fabulous literature – the *Arabian Nights* in particular. The extraordinary in exotic texts can shadow forth some gist in daily experience that I would have failed to recognize without its help. Coleridge gives (as an instance) the concept of 'Vastness', which he believes he could never have discovered in nature alone. Having acquired a sense of 'Vastness' through his reading of fiction, he does not get lost in detail when contemplating the night sky.

Sometimes I meet with concepts in literature that do not open up natural dimensions in this way – in Genesis, the concept of God and the concept of revelation. I read Genesis and meet with events that I do not really understand and which, in my shaming failure to understand, I wish to discredit.

Early one morning in late May, I look up a Dorset hillside and observe how a stone wall indicates a relationship to a tree. Wall and tree come together in mind. The conjunction has about it a sudden radiance which I do not understand. I mythologize the experience by thinking that, for a moment, I have glimpsed the gods. And I recall naturalistic anthropological theories which propose that early man first had experiences of this kind and in this way came to the concept of God. But this I find myself doubting. I think this is how lovers of nature sometimes sanction their love of nature – by thinking to discover the supernatural or some deeper essence in nature; but I suspect that this is a post-Romantic manner of thinking, very different from the revelations in Genesis. Revelation in Genesis is unequivocal. The Platonist and Augustinian clouds are parted. Accidentals in the world conjoin in my mind and I am tempted to give them a transcendental meaning. In Genesis the natural world is marginal to the revelation, which is explicit, absolute and not necessarily aesthetic.

Is my Dorset experience trivial – this lingering over the random conjunction of branch and sky? My seventeen-year-old self would have thought not. It would have thought that moments of natural revelation were important in any life and it would have pointed to favourite authors in support of this view. I am inclined to see this kind of experience as trivial now, largely because I think of the autobiographical uses of experience in general as trivial. On the other hand, if I allow myself to believe that the autobiographical is important, then this experience, which remains with me, must – by the fact of its insistence – be considered important. Autobiography depends on the fact that some experiences tug more at the memory than others.

What I find troubling about the idea of autobiography in general and this experience in particular (and what encourages me to see it as devoid of insight) is its emphasis on the self – and on the uniqueness of individual experience. I want to dismiss beliefs in the value of heightened perception as a rationalization of the adolescent's need to find thrills, in life, as though life were a constantly flagging entertainment.

To live for moments of thrill in a life largely made up of unthrilling moments is to pay a heavy price for the commitment. And it leaves unanswered the question as to what the aesthete should do with the unthrilling moments. Should they be given some sort of status in the golden pages of his autobiography, or should they be forgotten because they have the unfortunate handicap of being unassertive? A dandy's snobberies are formed from discriminations of this kind.

I want to drop the model of self and the other, whether Augustinian or empirical (the two are more closely connected, perhaps through puritanism, than I would like to admit: the empiricist, not least, tends to deny the relationship between the exercise of perception and guilt). I think that the empirical model of the interacting subject and object as a source for knowledge gives a false understanding of the ways in which symbolism comes about.

My seventeen-year-old self, setting store on epiphanies – and on the value of autobiographical reconstruction – would have found support for his beliefs in Ernst Cassirer's theory that the mythic imagination articulates itself, and self-evolvingly discovers manners of symbol, in three stages of awareness. Cassirer's mythic imagination first senses a generalized atmosphere of awe, which it defines as 'mana' – Ariel flickering like summer lightning between the masts of a ship. Then it senses beauty in the momentary: the drift of a branch across water. In memory the moment condenses into a vision of a God, which the mythic imagination feels compelled to name. Subsequently it seeks to name each stage of a work process with the names of different gods (Cassirer, 1950).

Genesis sees it more simply. God appears, and there is no doubt. When Jacob dreams of God, he believes that God actually appears before him. God's visitations require no prelude in nature and no symbolism of any kind. They are not displaced and not necessarily aesthetic and in no way related to accidental conjunctions in phenomena. Knowledge is never baffling in Genesis. God bluntly appears and speaks. He is without resonance or echo. He is not portentous.

Adam names the animals. Is this different from his naming of God? But Adam does not name God. God cannot be named, in the same way as he cannot be known. Adam is not allowed to name God. How then can God be designated? God is given very defined actions. He closes the doors of the Ark, for instance. When I name the animals, I perceive certain simple, even attractive, entities – the calf which licks my face may seem to invite a name. But God, like Zeus, is a baby only in some of his manifestations. If he does manifest himself as a baby in the New Testament, and I allow myself to approach him and realize my likeness to him, through Adam, I swiftly shrink away from him as I realize that I might have to live out his dreadful fate. God is both absolute creation and destruction, and woe betide anyone who becomes one of his disciples.

Portents

I cannot avoid a sense of portent. Some moments seem more significant than others, although I cannot readily say why. A sense of portent, of a Platonic nature, enters into the New Testament, often most evidently in its review of Old Testament experience. In the New Testament the practical travellings of the patriarchs gather to them an allusiveness of meaning and a music that the men of the Old Testament would have found unexpected. God had promised them immediate and reasonable satisfactions: the continuation of their line, the possession of a specific, necessary land. In the New Testament, the project has changed. The patriarchs are thought to have hungered for a continual and unseeable city, their aspirations to have become unworldly, insensible and Platonic. Revelation is no longer clear; it speaks in tongues that are not the tongues of the world. Its dreams cannot be interpreted in terms of available experiences.

Events that had appeared ordinary disclose themselves as portents. In a brief episode, Melchizedeck meets Abraham and offers him sustenance. Melchizedeck becomes a figure of unusual significance to the priesthood, resonant, intimating a half-heard music. Why should this moment, rather than any other, be endowed with significance? In the same way, perhaps as when I review my past, I find the events that are most memorable happen to emerge in my mind unpredictably. Life has the property of being meaningful in ways that its events do not seem to contain; and life writes the stories of our lives in ways that we often would not prefer.

Naturalistic accounts of God, whether in the Old Testament or in anthropological writings, distort the experience of people who do not think within the terms of naturalistic expectation. God is not an autobiographical event, nor an event that confirms the value of sensibility. His Old Testament existence obliterates any conception of autobiography or of personal experience. He denies symbolic strategies of this kind. If I set my experience at the centre of the universe, I will have to resort to metaphor to maintain and extend my descriptions. The patriarchs would have experienced life as both simpler and other: they did not have to twist about experience to suit their preference. They would have seen what they had to see, quite literally.

8

A door in the sun

MY FEELINGS tell me that as a post-Renaissance man, I cannot avoid the semi-empirical, semi-Romantic model of the self investigating a knowable other as crucial to my thinking. But such a model is bound up with a centring on selfhood and with residues of a puritan ethos that I distrust and even fear.

In Genesis I recognize an older way of describing experience. In it all coherence seems to lie with an other who is essentially unknowable and who has all the powers of action. In psychoanalytic terms, I may describe the unknowable other in terms of those life and death forces which I think to buffet the ego-to-be, the foetus in a state of fluctuation between life and death.

This contrast between a defence, which is perhaps a species of autism – the self as egotistic in its perceptions – and the condition of utter helplessness which it defends against, are hard to sort out, one from the other; and I am not sure that I can sort them out to anyone's satisfaction.

But I am touching on an important and widely experienced creative tension, and I ask the reader to share my sense of frustration. My concern is to focus on the tension itself rather than on its polarities. As so often in such tensions, words switch meanings easily, often taking on their opposite meaning. I think the struggle to describe the nature of this polarity – between pre-birth helplessness and later egotism – is important in any attempt to escape from triviality into those deep truths in feelings that inform the question: what is the meaning of life?

The fact that I am helpless does not entail abandoning any authority I may have to make moral decisions to those who claim to be the guardians of received truth. And yet if I protest against the priesthoods, élites and academies, as I do, I will find myself once more alone and faced by the need to find a method, as perhaps Descartes was. I will face once more the pressures that would have me retreat into egotism and the need to extemporize moralities in the manner I call allegorical.

The individual conscience

Descartes doubted the value of any knowledge received on trust. He observed rope-makers and cooks and sailors at work: he wished to feel on the pulse how others underwent experience. When he came to learn about human anatomy, he did not rely on text books – he insisted on carrying out his own dissections. Scientific experiment interested him as an activity into which he himself could enter; otherwise it did not interest him at all.

His creative use of egotism was characteristic of the Renaissance. Knowledge was meaningful to the extent that it could be transacted through mind. His *Meditations* of 1641 takes the form of a semi-secular *Pilgrim's Progress* (1678) – and in many ways it anticipates the magnification of moral scruple that occurs in psychoanalysis. In a religious manner, it supposes antagonists and temptations and moral progressions in thought. It is unlike the revelation that (I assume)

Adam experienced when he first opened his eyes: the flooding of absolutely everything into a wholly vulnerable foetal-like being (the ultimate birth experience, perhaps). Descartes in his contemplation is critical, evaluatory, in quest for a method or a narrative to understanding.

Truth is no longer the prerogative of priesthoods. It has to be verified through personal experience, through conscience. (Such a belief is a remarkably recent one.) Descartes was inclined to take little for granted. The Holy Spirit had abandoned the sacraments; Jacob's stone no longer seeped knowledge; fetishes had lost their power; and the intellectual priesthood could no longer conduct rites without question. The self had to immerse itself in the element; to drown in the conditions of its own experience – to pass through some anguishing process of symbolic death in order to achieve the living truth. Acts of introspection had become meaningful as possible ways to truthfulness; painful self-examination, with an emphasis on the individuality of the human heart, took on an unusual importance – and not only in French culture.

The art of living

'Puritan autobiographies,' claims Owen C. Watkins, writing of the English Puritans,

> were the product of a Puritan conviction that the highest art a man could practise was the art of living . . . The only masterpiece worthy of the name was to be achieved in the most complex and difficult of all forms of creative endeavour: a human life. (Watkins, 1972, p. 1)

Immersing yourself in the element is dangerous, a form of dying, a possible losing of the self in the object of its discovery. Descartes distanced himself when he contemplated the work of the rope-makers – unlike John Bunyan, who allowed himself a more disturbing withinness when he eavesdropped on the women of Bedford.

> I came where there was [sic] three or four poor women sitting at a door in the Sun, and talking about the things of

61

God; and being now willing to hear them discourse, I drew near to hear what they said; for I was now a brisk talker also my self in the matter of religion: but now I may say, *I heard, but I understood not*; for they were far above out of my reach, for their talk was about a new birth, the work of God on their hearts, also how they were convinced of their miserable state by nature. (Bunyan, 1666, p. 14)

The priest finds himself witness to a Yawistic phenomenon – God's breathing into Adam's mouth – and it may destroy him. Bunyan found himself in a similar condition, though unlike Adam he had some power to make a choice. He could still reject God. The door might be a door in the sun as well as a door in sunlight, the door to a Platonic glare that burns away the deception of the senses.

Hard to distinguish God's breathing into Adam's mouth from compulsion. Bunyan was afflicted by nightmares, and his tongue turned to blasphemy. (It is as though his tongue could not curb his need to be ravished and engulfed by uncensorable words: perhaps turning to obscenity was evidence of his God-given literary gifts.) He sought to play the innocent ball game of 'cat' and 'A voice did suddenly dart from Heaven into my Soul, which said, *Wilt thou leave thy sins, and go to Heaven? or have thy sins, and go to Hell?*' (Bunyan, 1666, p. 10).

Peering into the imaginary zone of the breast, realm of the mythic imagination, the infant discovers monsters within that prohibit creative play. The baby immersed in the breast has to face up to persecutors within and without. In the breast it can find super-ego elements, totemic phantoms, screamings, evidences of a murderous coupling. This is as though to look over an imaginary cliff-edge and to let your feet give way.

God's spies

The making of a life and the making of an autobiography are virtually synonymous, if we think of both as wrought. A meaning imposed on life – making oneself into something – or a meaning drawn from life: the two questions can barely be distinguished. I am made, or I allow myself to be made. Doubting the priesthood and its wrought symbolisms within myself, I have to look to the Holy Spirit as a primary source in experience.

'Quest: How do I know the word to be the word?' asked the Puritan Richard Sibbes:

> Ans: It carrieth proof and evidence in itself. It is an evidence that the fire is hot to him that feeleth it, and that the sun shineth to him that looks on it; how much more doth the word . . . I am sure I felt it, it warmed my heart, and converted me. (Sibbes, 1863, vol. iv, p. 363)

Having the sun on my face may allow me to doubt the meaning of any sense communication and to suppose, as Descartes did, that the meaning of my experience is dependent on some internal index of truthfulness. Appreciating the experience appears to be bound up with appreciating something that is not primarily given to the senses.

Reading a book about watch-making does not necessarily convey to me how the act of watch-making transforms the self. Lear's implied belief that observing the poorest people in his kingdom has revealed the mystery of things to him foreshadows John Bunyan's listening to the poor women 'sitting at a door in the Sun'. Experiencing the world, directly rather than by hearsay, can uncover non-worldly meanings. Sucking at the breast encourages us to look within: both into ourselves and into the imaginary realms that the breast contains. Puritan autobiography is about the struggle with sin, confession, the hope for grace, the discovery of the eternal city: a topography for life's journey.

Experience – it is implied – shifts us from egocentricity. We no longer spy on things from our own point of view. Lear in captivity clandestinely aligns himself with the unknown and helpless spiritual realm. He invites Cordelia to

> take upon's the mystery of things
> As if we were God's spies.
>
> (V. iii. 16–17)

'God's spies', alluding possibly to recusant priests in hiding, poses a threat to the legitimate order. In turn, a spiritual order, often in necessary concealment, threatens the political orthodoxy: it works by stealth. Political establishments activate an illegitimate power: claims to legitimacy appear to precipitate illegitimate aspirations. Shakespeare, wily politician, thinks that spying, though wicked, can be used in the service of the good – or at least in the service of the expedient. Goodness must conceal itself as though it were in some Platonist fable, or like Edgar, or Moses in the bullrushes. Cordelia does not conceal herself, and she is destroyed.

> The oldest hath borne most: we, that are young,
> Shall never see so much nor live so long.
>
> (V. iii. 323–5)

Survival, in the sense of being able continuously to be responsive to suffering, is thought admirable. But then in *King Lear* the fact of having survived a length of time is thought admirable in itself. This is to assert, extraordinarily, that to reach a great age is evidence of virtue: one has weathered so many storms, if only by surviving so many transitions in development; human beings finding a prototype for the passing of existence through them in the 'suffering' or distress of weathered trees and ancient stones. Endurance uncovers its source in persistence, the lasting out of an organism in time, the virtue that relates man to things.

Abandoning the commitment to endure undermines virtue. Suicide is a recurrent motif in *King Lear*. It is gesture of a kind that halts continuance. In the most beautiful scene in the play, Edgar plays a therapeutic trick on his father, Gloucester, by conducting him through an imaginary act of self-annihilation. He creates an imaginary cliff-drop in the blind man's mind, into which the blind man naturally cannot pitch himself. It is an exercise in temptation, like Descartes's meeting with his antagonist; a commando's training for battle; and the parallel with the pilgrim in his progress – Adam tempted in the garden, Christ in the desert – is

64

unavoidable. In psychoanalysis, too, many of the possibilities that would kill you in the actual world can be lived through fairly safely in the transference, in ways that lead to an enhanced sense of life. It is as though Shakespeare himself thought of his plays as cliff-drops into which an audience, in identification with Gloucester in his blindness, thinks to fall to a symbolic death, only to be reborn again.[1]

To some extent, Gloucester dies, since through his mortifying failure to kill himself he loses the impulse to commit suicide. He dies symbolically and is reborn again, within the same flesh; expelled from the old priesthood and initiated into a new one, which consists of the world's illegitimate congregation, the poor and dispossessed.

Goodness in a world of sorrows must find ways of reincarnating itself in order to survive: thus Edgar is goodness veiled, the truth concealed, the God glimpsed in the drift of branches over water. Goodness must enter into fictions to reveal its heart, and self-dramatize its opportunities. Edgar helps his father to practise the subterfuges of endurance, by transfiguring the dumbness of utter despair into a family story, about an imaginary devil, complex in appearance, and about events that populate the ups-and-downs of an imaginary busy cliff. The beauty of the scene lies in its detaching of pain from cruel motive, its Buddhistic serenity being spacious in its sense of portent.

Common sense would support suicide under certain circumstances. In *King Lear*, suicide is denied its Roman honour: only Edmund dies by his own conniving – and miserably. In its way, *King Lear* speaks for the sufferings of life at its most primal – it speaks for the foetus in the travails of birth.

Undergoing birth, in so far as we have been allowed to undergo it, by inner or outer sanction, provides me with a precedent for the need to endure without question, and to survive. If the foetus were to commit suicide, assuming it had that power, it might endanger its mother. This is one reason why suicide invites discouragement: in destroying myself, I destroy the world.

The 'ripeness' which Edgar thinks 'is all' is birth itself, the fulfilling of the fruit; which in King Lear becomes the journey into death, as though birth and death were identical rites of passage, or priestly initiations, through a never-ending series of similar states: the endurings of life are elaborations on the endurings of pregnancy. Gordon Craig designed a setting for *King Lear* – an arched wattle-covered walkway that presciently alluded to the birth journey or the tunnel with a light at the end, an image which, it is sometimes said, the dying dream about.[2]

The foetus within the infant, by the fact of having undergone childbirth experientially, is competent to recognize that God's covenant anticipates the contract of the birth labour: the covenant being my need to endure the creativity of others in their act of making myself, to risk death in the act of becoming a born being – that most precarious of existents, an individual. Lear divests himself of his priestly trappings to experience once again the exigencies of being born. Seeing so much and living so long is a process that hallows, like the birth process, a rite of passage whose enduring grants life. All enduring would seem to outwit Herod and the other antagonists to our birth.

With hindsight, Lear's regal divestment can be seen as catastrophically wise. No longer king or priest sunk in hierarchy and received meanings – so caught up in the process of symbolization that he has become a symbol himself – he must feel and think things anew in a process of continuous rebirth. Old men as explorers travel out – like newborns.

The revelation of experience shadows forth a mystery which God's spies may observe. Acknowledging the mystery displaces the observer from the centre of perception. Consciousness has authority, but its authority is only marginal.

The divestment of Lear

Being immersed in the element, depending on God's breath, the Yawistic experience – the primary religious experience of

helplessness, of being awesomely reborn, again and again –
emerges from a level before ideas of the self and non-self have
been separated. Adam and God share the same lungs. Insight
is constant in its being pulsed by God into the foetus: the
infant has no power to maintain the pulse, no available
notation to formalize the shock of revelation.

The view of the priest in the self, with its steadying of
fluctuations in meaning, does not illuminate the mysterious
process by which the spirit acquires the letter. 'The spirit that
makes the word effectual, doth by that efficacy convince the
soul that the word is the word' (Sibbes, 1863, vol. iv, p. 363).
The notation hardens; or rather the reading of the received
text loses any truth. The priest in the self no longer serves the
vision; it claims to be the guardian of the spirit, or even the
spirit itself. It murders all rivals.

Harpo

A man, who has recently entered therapy, dreams that he is
attending synagogue with his girl-friend. There is no separation of the sexes. He finds himself sitting next to his
girl-friend in the room that he thinks of as the main place of
worship. The other people in the room are shadowy – he is
aware of the sombre and formal nature of their clothes. He
wanders into another room; here, the people are casually
dressed, in sports jackets, shirts open at the neck. He goes
into another space, possibly an outside space, with high
walls. In spite of himself, he is drawn into playing cricket – or
is it football? The players are led by a blond curly-haired
man, who reminds him of one of the Marx brothers. Is it
Chico – the one who plays the harp? No, he corrects himself,
the harpist and the leader of the team must be Harpo.

He goes back to the first room and cannot find his
girl-friend. He associates the three spaces in the dream to
three rooms in a medieval castle or to three places in a small
walled city.

The confusing of two of the Marx brothers – the two who
play musical instruments, that is, and the forgetting of

Harpo's name – is a possible route into the dream experience. In playing the harp, Harpo seems to immerse himself in the music, in the strings of the harp itself. He is inside something, so much so that he seems unable to discriminate outward or worldly signs. He cannot read the worldly signs – and happily does not know whom to be deferential to. All desirable blondes are the same to him.

The patient wanted to get better at making decisions. He had come into therapy in order to work out a problem; reasonably, he had expected therapy to help him in the world. He now found that of its own accord the therapeutic experience was drawing him into something else, both attractive and dangerous, an unworldly condition where he would no longer be safe. He had begun to forget his initial desire to have his problems solved and began to enjoy therapy for its own sake.

The experience of being nurtured – he was beginning to realize – compels the self to move in certain directions without itself being under direction. He clearly had a talent for dreaming and for appreciating imaginative moves in dream interpretation. His talent had no immediate source in his environment or upbringing. He wanted to resist his wish to talk about his dreams, as though to resist a possible love affair. His incipient passion for dreaming and for the understanding of dreams might consume him.

An adult in precarious adulthood, who has denied that his former infant self has continued neglectedly to survive within him, allows himself to return to states of infancy – even to those states where self and non-self cannot be differentiated. Unfortunately – he fears – he finds that he has lost his apparently adult self and must remain in dreaded infancy for ever. The anthropologist visits a disturbing, fascinating primitive place and loses any ability to return home; he must accept his condition, as a vulnerable native among natives. A historian travels in mind into the sixteenth century and finds that he can no longer be an antiquarian; he is forever trapped in the past, in the climate of witchcraft and witch persecution; he cannot return to his former pseudo-adult self.

The patient dresses correctly. He keeps danger at a distance. In worldly terms he is successful. Gaunt and priest-like, he takes off his jacket and shining shoes at the beginning of the session and disposes them by the couch, as though conducting a religious ceremony. Ostensibly, he does not want to rumple his jacket or mess the couch with his immaculate shoes. His dream indicates a different meaning for divestment. To immerse himself in the object, he has to move through a transitory stage, the room in which people are casually dressed.

Clearly the gap between immersing yourself in the element, losing yourself in the object and being outside (and conscious of demarcations) was immense, as great as the difference in the cultural conditions of the Middle Ages and the present world. He had associated the synagogue to a medieval castle. He thought that leaving the consulting-room might be as disquieting as having to leave a medieval castle for the modern world.

I have an experience – or rather the experience immerses me in its element. I am Adam breathed into by God. I am so lost in the experience that I have no means to notate it.

At what point does the spirit begin to acquire the letter? A child immersed in the element makes a drawing. She does not appear to reach out for expressiveness. The notation is to hand, as are words in her mouth or dreams in her sleep. There is no necessary connection between her having the experience and the experience having an appreciable meaning.

Harpo within the harp. The depth of the immersion in experience appears to effect the different uses of memory and notation. If I have a 'deep' experience, I may forget it until I have another 'deep' experience like it. Eliot writes in the *Four Quartets* about music being heard so deeply that it is not heard at all – 'but you are the music/While the music lasts'.

Notes

1 In primitive thinking, in which there is no theory of gravitation, the vista in Gloucester's mind's eye is of an object that disintegrates the observer. You do not smash through falling on to the beach: the beach rises up and hits you. It is a little like being drawn into Edgar Allan Poe's maelstrom (Poe, 1899, vol. 1, pp. 150–67). Unlike Jacob's stone – a pillow which feeds dreams of plenitude into the sleeper – the vista projects disintegration into you. The God who guarantees your potency through dreams is the God who smashes in your skull by flying up a boulder at you. It is the God who gives you a vision of death (which some of the Romantic poets can find sublime).

2 'It was at this very moment that Ivan Ilyich had fallen through the hole and caught sight of the light, and it was revealed to him that his life had not been what it ought to have been' (Tolstoy, 1960, p. 160).

9

The uses of egocentricity

For man to tell how human life began
Is hard; for who himself beginning knew?
(Paradise Lost 8:250)

I BEGIN at the beginning and go on right through to the end. But where exactly do I begin? Do I begin with my own consciousness and my first experiences of nurture within the womb of the family; or do I begin with some impersonal diagrammatic account of the universe – the containments of the Aristotelian and Newtonian universe, for instance; or should I be like the famous Jewish theologians of ancient Alexandria who dazzled and defeated the philosophers in argument by resolutely beginning and ending every discourse with the unknowable concept of God?[1]

When I read Genesis I want to be like the Jewish theologians, and to start from some point remote from self-centred concerns, a point that is both unknowable and unnameable. But I cannot escape my very personal entanglement with nature and a body-derived consciousness. The provisional model I revert to, and which many people work with, whether true or not, has self-consciousness at its centre like a pool of light and moves out to take in, with a steadily increasing obscurity, the whole of mankind.

The model has immediate bearing on the experience of infancy and childhood. I see the world as beginning in myself and its boundaries, then around it my family and its boundaries, then my school, and eventually the rest of the world. The model places me at the centre of the world, as though I were the baby in the manger – as though I were the hallowed child. I do not think it is possible to be self-centred without thinking of myself as God. Giving up the delusional belief that I am God for the belief that I may be able to relate to some spark of divinity is not easy.

One (damaging) way out of self-centredness is to blank out any concern with kinship. Some people show little interest in the thoughts and feelings of their parents or grandparents, or in their family history or in the history of their fellow human beings. The patient referred to on p. 40 seemed to be incurious about the lives of his near relatives. He seldom referred to them; and when he did, spoke of them indifferently. I found him elusive. I was unable to imagine his experiences in babyhood, except by tentative inference. I think he must have always lived in a condition of suspicion, thinking of his relatives as predators to be fended off. His one vivid memory of his mother was of having found her once lying on her bed in a state of drunkenness. She was defenceless; and he was able to have a perception of her. I could not tell whether he thought he had damaged her. Or whether he had been frightened by the sight, or triumphant, or what; I do not know. He did not show his hand on many issues. He was intelligent; he preferred to be dissociated from his intelligence.

Possibly he had projected so much of his disowned self into his relatives that he was unable to tolerate them as people other than himself, as people with lives that related to his own. I think of an eminent painter who had been very poor and was taken up by rich clients. The painter cut himself off from his past in every way and sought to destroy every picture from the earlier period. He seemed unable to discriminate good from bad in his former life. He had undergone a conversion, and all the bad had been left in the past. My patient had been through a similar conversion. When his wife gave birth to their first baby, he sought to get rid of me. I had become the recipient of his badness. He wanted to present himself as the sinner washed clean at the infant's cot. He wanted to get rid of his feelings of unworthiness.

I ask myself: how far am I like my parents or grand-parents? I want to answer this question in terms of genetic inheritance, although (so far as I know) the question is not possibly answerable on present knowledge. I prefer the genetic to the phenomenological approach as being the less painful and use the genetic question to half-conceal a painful issue: how far is my interest in my progenitors an extension of my own self-centredness? Milton writes from within a centre in his self, but without being self-centred. His point of departure is different from that of Spinoza, say, whose ethical system begins in some imagining of otherness, not unlike the non-conscious, non-experiential deity-otherness of Genesis.

Knowing myself at the beginning

In *Paradise Lost*, Milton imagines the thoughts that Adam might have had on first opening his eyes. He raises questions that do not occur in Genesis, concerned as he is with a concept of experience in which transmissions of consciousness are of central importance. Miltonic experience is more than sensation or perception or unconscious enactment. It involves sophisticated notations, the uses of literacy, to register the unique and precious elements in selfhood. It dwells on the connection between the values of selfhood and literacy; at almost any cost, it must assess the nuances in feeling that make up the self.

Having experiences in this sense entails the registering of experiences, if only in thought. Obviously, the sharing of experiences would include the sharing and registering of experiences within myself, in the continuous soliloquy unfolding within me that fears death as the snuffing out of the whole romantic enterprise of selfhood.

In the puritan conscience, tales always have tellers; they are always held to be accountable tales, justifiable in their ways. The mind acts as a library of narratives and tales to be shared – generation by generation, through families and nations. Societies have a past and future that take on a usable meaning through the concept of recordable experience. What did my father think and feel when he was young? What does my infant think and feel? Why should the Miltonic question of my having inspiration be related to the sufferings and insights of our primal parents, the originators of mankind? On one level, informative questions; on another, depressed, allegorical, haunted by the desire to be known.

Accountable though I am for my thoughts, in some strange Augustinian way I am also to be held accountable for the thoughts of others. Augustine believes that Eve's transgression influences each subsequent generation, with increasing debit. In the puritan imagination, the significance of consciousness as a governing element in life begins to gain fruition.

What did Adam first see – what does anyone of us first see? Milton does not think that the problems of perception and recollection in infancy might be dissimilar from those of an adult born into full maturity. His Adam is typical of the human condition. Like the rest of us, he can be held responsible for the condition of conscience.

Waking into awareness, as might any of us, 'from soundest sleep,' Milton's Adam finds himself in a state of sweat – and lying on 'the flowery herb' (*Paradise Lost* 8:254–5). A shipwrecked mariner wakes to consciousness on some unfamiliar island: he might be a sleeping beauty, awaking from a thousand years of sleep.

He sweats. The sun dries him out. He is able to enjoy the beautiful landscape about him. He finds himself mysteriously able to speak and to describe his surroundings. It occurs to him that he must have been made by some great maker. He falls asleep and dreams of a shape divine – an angel perhaps, or God himself – who leads him up a hill and shows him the garden of bliss. He yearns, in dream, to eat fruit from well-endowed trees. He awakes from dream to find the dream experience enacted in reality: here before him is the garden of bliss and the tempting trees.

He awoke and found it truth: Keats will see this type of realization as imaginative.[2] Suffering feelings he does not understand, pangs of loneliness, Adam dreams of Eve and wakes to find her before him. God vouchsafes the importance of dreaming by replicating his dream in actuality. The capacity to dream underlies perception; as Santayana thought, we dream in order to perceive. A God-function in mind, which enables us to dream, enables us to perceive – not just anything; it enables us to perceive the unique qualities of Eve.

Milton (and Keats also) describe a process of symbolic aspiration uncharacteristic of Genesis. It is a way of thinking that is more typical of the later Platonic and Christian commentaries on Genesis, as in the Epistle to the Hebrews.

> By faith he became a sojourner in the land of promise, as in a land not his own, dwelling in tents with Isaac and Jacob, the heirs with him of the same promise: for he looked for the city which hath the foundations, whose builder and maker is God. (11:9–10)

Adam dreams of Eve and then, on awaking, discovers her to be there, created by God. The mind looks inwardly for its object and having found its inward object discovers the object in actuality. Miltonic mind does not realize its own visions: it is God who makes the vision actual. In Genesis, God is like some process in mind which denies or reverses symbol formation. (Bion's beta function perhaps.) In *Paradise Lost* God is the symbol-making presence in the imagination which underwrites the truthfulness of the perception of the object. Adam does not hallucinate the object. Eve is a presence no human mind could have hallucinated. The truth value of the vision is guaranteed by God's presence in Adam's mind.[3]

Paradise is now; or rather, Milton allows paradise momentarily to have been realized for his primal father, in the paradisal gardens themselves. By implication such realizations continue to recur in mind, through mind's amazing capacity for symbolization – Plato's wonderful discovery that minds are actually Platonic and capable of Platonic (symbolizable, articulated) moments of ecstasy. Milton's Adam awakes to an Eve-world and can say: I had already dreamt of your existence. Adam is the first Puritan Pilgrim Father, yearning that an America of the mind should become actual. Forever we live in hopes to awake and find it truth. Forever we awake and do, if we are so mindful, find it truth. Such processes of symbolization really got under way with the Fall and the beginnings of history. But for Milton (though not for the authors of Genesis) the essentials of symbolic process were already established through the fact of Eve's birth. (This is how I understand the myth.)

In Milton, the question of personality takes the form of Adam dreaming of Eve. Adam is not blank at the time of her creation. Eve is part of his interior; she exists in the climate of his mind. She is the 'tale' of his life and the tale exists within the atmosphere of the teller. Out of the 'tale' of his life will unfold children and their children: murder, ambition and the flowering of the seed.

I think that being aware of the 'flavour' of consciousness in the story is an equivalent for the infant of being aware of its mother's personality and disposition while it feeds: the fragrance of her body, the look in her eyes, the nature of her hair and skin – of clothing, of changing shape. The question of personality is related to 'flavours' within the self, ironies, the sense of accrued or accruing experience. Dreams, too, exist in an atmosphere often associated with the smell, sight, taste or touch of a mother's body. Clues of this kind attract in this way or that, as we listen to the story, enhancing the sense we already have of an actual and rightful place in existence. Anecdotes about our parents or grandparents or often imaginary ancestors, like Lear, have deep currents, often hidden in a clause. They pull in this way or that.

In Genesis it matters not who tells the tale. In *Paradise Lost* we must trust the teller, or at least have some sense of Milton's selfhood and history, to understand the tale. A narrative concerned with ancient events meaningfully keeps returning to Milton himself and his anguish over inspiration, as though the need to return were a central clue to the meaning of the poem.

Certain kinds of transmission are necessarily bathed in personality. Milton's anguished doubts about whether he is inspired or not are crucial to his historical interests. He needs to understand the story of Adam – as he needs to understand the story of Britain, or the story of his parents' lives – in order to make sense of his own experiences. His Adam has to exist in the liquid suspension of a mind to understand the presence of Eve.

Similarly, in order to thrive, mind needs nurture, the love that parents can give their children. Adam needs that sort of beginning. The archangels who instruct Adam act as inter-mediaries for the parents Adam did not have. They are parents whose parenting creates forms of mind. They embody those angelic arcades in mental space which we call past and future. No stone seeps meaning into this Adam's head: he is no Genesis patriarch.

The archangels cannot tell Adam about his infancy; they can tell him, though, about the creation of the universe; and they can show him the future, as though in a dream. The archangels allow Adam to experience past and future imagin-atively – as shared social thoughts.

Social life and family lore shared with younger and older members of the family increase the dimensions of conscious-ness. My grandfather's successes and failures become my successes and failures. His meeting with a great man brings honour to me, my children and their children. The places where my grandfathers went to are familiar in my imagina-tion, and more vivid now, than the setting in which I find myself at present. So too in fiction. Lear's heath becomes my heath; and when I think of the cliffs of Dover, I think of Gloucester's cliff, which never existed, except in a poet's eye. Shakespeare's imaginary cliff is for me the surest bit of England.

Stories are not secure in one generation: they are like the Ark that crossed the Flood.

Notes

1 The superiority of Scripture to philosophy is brought out dramatically by the author of the *Letter of Aristeas* in his account of the table-talk between the Jewish sages and King Ptolemy Philadelphus. The king asks these Jewish sages all kinds of questions. They answer each question. But the common recurrent refrain in all their answers, expressing the same sentiment in different words, is that God is the source of everything we know and everything we do. Thereupon, says the author, 'with loud voice the king greeted them all and spoke kindly to them, and all those who were present expressed their approval, especially the Jewish sages, for they were far superior to the philosophers both in conduct and argument, since they always made God the starting-point. (Wolfson, 1947, vol. i, p. 27)

2 'The Imagination may be compared to Adam's dream – he awoke and found it truth' (Letter to Benjamin Bailey, 22 November 1817; cited in Forman, 1952, p. 67).

3 This view of perception would be opposed by the psychoanalytic inference that if God makes Eve at the moment when Adam dreams of her, then God and Adam are probably components of the same mind; or, alternatively, that the child Adam who dreams of its mother in persistent intercourse with its father, and on waking finds her reassuringly with him, is able to presume that he, Adam, was his mother's lover. Both these formulations, which misuse psychoanalysis, take the tension and interest out of Keats's idea.

Part II

Enough for us to take as certain that when a man is able to think about the nature of his own mind, he will discover the truth nowhere else than in himself. And he will discover not something he did not know but something he had not thought about.

Augustine, The Trinity, Book 4:8

10

Stories

WE TELL stories to each other. Ark stories, transmissions defending the imagination against the Deluge or the Fall. Listening to family stories as a child, I felt there was a special resonance about them. There was curiosity about my parents' insides, of course, about the atmosphere of their emotional inheritance, and how they had come together and brought about my being – these were issues that made some impression. But there was also puzzlement: how did things fit together? Many of the stories were about ancestors in ceaseless movement, emigrants and pilgrims, seekers after new lands and continuing cities. They certainly had it harder than I did. I was shaken, when visiting the *Cutty Sark*, to see the kind of quarters my sailing-ship grandfather must have inhabited. Over the years anecdotes were mulled over and meanings looked for that might increase the meaning of my own existence. The lives of the dead were looked to for allegorical significance: I wanted the meaning printed out.

I think that this was evidence of depression. So many

people get lost. In the end all of us get lost. Memories of ancestors fade into nothingness as they recede in time.

The stories my parents or one of my grandfathers told me were very related to the qualities of their personalities. I thought to see things through their eyes. But there were other stories that seemed to spring from nowhere, like the world that first faced Adam, stories without a narrative tone or governing consciousness: fairy tales, children's songs and games, many kinds of dream, the narrative of Genesis itself.

Pastness can be thought of as a space in the present. In my imagination, I see the past as like the obscure Congo river in Conrad's *Heart of Darkness*: Plotinus lives one station upstream. Journeys into the past occur on a map on which distances in time become distances in space. A country, like a family, exists in time as a kind of space, in a space notable for its losses. When the old house is broken up, we lose a fragment of our past – as well as a familiar place. When mother or father sink beneath the ground, they take with them an unrecorded inheritance, their bodies being tabernacles of a lost knowledge. I shall never know this or that cherishable fact about the family past because I did not ask the right question at the right time.

With the passing of years, the dead who move about in my mind discard any biographical data they might have had. They are no longer beings in history who inhabit facts. And their successors are no longer able to recollect stories about them. But they continue to be aching presences in thought, abstract powers, immensely persuasive, banging about in a space which I am inclined to identify with another kind of imaginary space, the vacant picture I have of their life-span.

I count out the dates of their births and their deaths on my fingers, as though my life depended on it. How long or short was the duration of this or that existence! Life-spans are all the long-lost dead have for me, remissions against the inevitable sentence. I think of my mariner grandfather in a small sailing-ship, some Noah in a biscuit tin, tossed about on the high seas.

In Dorset I am aware of an unobtrusive and ubiquitous fact. Everywhere there are graveyards and gravestones marking out names and life-spans (these are often very brief). Other people's ancestors: and yet the living imagination curiously and without narcissistic intent appropriates them as though they were its own. In Dorset the past is so close, in London so safely distant. I prefer the city: it mediates and distracts the mysterious pains of kinship.

Albion

Existing so, in mental space as well as time, the idea of England arises out of these conditions, into a spaceless, timeless idealized condition that we might call Albion: an idea in the mind indistinguishable from Canaan, where unknown ancestors, as well as known ones, forever live. Milton realized that the early history of Britain contained many blanknesses into which mythologies might enter. He thought these mythologies should be recorded, even though historically untrue.

Mythologies of pastness concern me as essential elements in health. Filling a blankness within me, I find the sons of Japheth – who many thought were founders of our race – or old Lear, figures who ceaselessly move (like my two actual grandfathers, the sea captain of Danish descent and the emigrant Scot who became a champion cyclist, in my mind as restlessly roaming as underworld shades). In terms of saga, of our need to transact with the largely unknown that meets us at every moment, Blake's belief that his ancestors were descended from a tribe of Israel, Noah's offspring, the sons of Japheth, is meaningful. In order to live with any fullness, I need to make a covenant with an idea that is both immeasurably powerful and unknowable. The idea cannot be proved: it is, as Coleridge says, its own evidence.

Parents tell stories out of a desire to share pastness with their children. Perhaps, too, they feel themselves to be nonentities before the child in the fullness of its originality. They wish to demonstrate that they are not like Adam,

newborn in adulthood, without a past or inwardness. They
may fear to damage the child by showing it that they have
survived some deluge, or undergone great suffering. But they
bear witness to the developmental, even in their moments of
fear.[1]

Primitively, they may think: I am fallen man. How can I be
an agent for goodness to my child; how can I represent, if at
all, the idea of a primal ancestor in sacred, timeless contract
with the source of his creation – and how far is it true to say
that I am bound seamlessly to the God who creates and
destroys absolutely?

Telling stories about the past can distance me from a sense
of sacred nowness, an Adam-engulfing which makes me feel
non-existent. In myth, you and I are descended from Adam
and identified with him. In Adam I die and live. Adam's
encounter with the unknown, with the mysterious powerful
idea that creates and destroys him – his covenant with the
idea – is the story the Bible tells again and again, although the
Adam figure in the encounter keeps re-appearing under
different guises.[2]

Notes

1 Bruno Bettelheim (1987, ch. 12) has written movingly about the
difficulties facing children who have to contain the idea of their
parents as having suffered intensely, and perhaps with heroism,
during times of war.

2 Many scholars have raised important conjectures about the
nature of the primal split in sensibility often implied in Creation
myths.

In some remarkable lectures given in Oxford in 1924, N. P.
Williams indicates how the Deluge cycle of myths and the Fall
cycle describe two variant theories of the primal split. The
Deluge cycle, which the Bible cryptically alludes to in a passage
placed before the Noah story (Genesis 6:1–4), concerns the
marriage of the sons of God (also known as the Angels or the
Watchers) and the daughters of men. This marriage entails the
misappropriation of divine power, and the emergence of chaos

and of monster peoples. Indeed, the mingling of 'the divine essence' with 'the seed of man' introduces the principle of evil into humanity. In various pseudepigraphic texts – most notably the Ethiopic *Book of Enoch* and the fragments of the *Book of Noah* – there is further evidence that the fallen Angels, or Watchers, 'corrupted the human race by imparting to it knowledge which the Creator had not meant it to possess. Here we detect the emergence of the motif which reappears in the second Fall-Story, that of Adam and Eve, and is closely paralleled by the Greek legend of Prometheus' (Williams, 1927, p. 25). It is probable that the Noah cycle of myths precedes the Adam cycle, which may account for the blanknesses and absences in the Adam story. If you imagine Adam to be Noah, then the perfect world that Adam awakes to in fact would be a delusion held against the recognition that Adam, as Noah, has awoken to a world largely destroyed in some universal Deluge.

For reasons unknown, the Adam story superseded the story of the Angels. Dr Williams thinks that the pious were revolted by the idea of sexual intercourse between celestial spirits and the daughters of men. Interestingly, the theological notion of 'concupiscence', which it anticipates, still informs the popular belief in original sin as identifiable with sex. 'We shall have occasion to note resemblances, sometimes slight and sometimes superficial, and sometimes astonishingly exact, between the idea of "concupiscence", as it appears in Jewish and Christian thought, and the Freudian conception of libido' (Williams, 1927, p. 35).

To each his own taste. For me, at any rate, the Genesis 6:4 account of the Watchers' relationship with the fair daughters of men is beautiful in its cherishing of ancestral achievement: 'There were giants of the earth in those days; and also after that, when the sons of God came unto the daughters of men, and they bare children to them, the same became mighty men which were of old, men of renown.'

11

Adam and Noah

GENESIS mythologizes an immense power and uncovers this power in history. The God of absolute creation is the God of absolute destruction. But how do I come to know this fact in the present moment? At one moment – the moment of the Flood – the absolute God, who created the world, destroys nearly all life on earth. 'And all flesh died that moved upon the earth' (7:21). A fact about the world. It may be a fact about mind, too, if I believe that mind has some impersonal substrate where absolute powers, of life and death, of creation and destruction, reign.

The story of Adam and the story of Noah are two sides of the same coin. The Bible scholar, Claus Westermann, writes:

> There is a far reaching parallel between the creation of humans and the flood narrative. Both begin with a decision of God about humanity, both envisage the possibility of the failure of humanity as God's creation; both are concerned with the existence or non-existence of humanity. Flood narrative and creation narrative (of humans) are

from the start obviously interrelated; they complement each other. (Westermann, 1984, p. 393)

Westermann points to the Flood story's relationship to other salient Genesis motifs, all of them pluralistic in tendency and threatening to monistic beliefs – motifs concerning the origins of civilization, marriages between humans and demideities, tower-building, the scatterings of races and the multiplications of languages:

The flood narrative is so central to the primeval event that each of the remaining primeval motifs can look to it as the focal point. This becomes even clearer when in a number of cases the flood narrative is identical with the creation narrative. (Westermann, 1984, p. 402)

The God of the Imagination reveals the fundamental unity in all differences. Myths circle and broach and genuflect to the power of this idea, while at the same time cushioning our approaches to it. Myths are like thoughts in a mind arrested at some point in development, ancient mariners having to tell the same story again and again, in the hope of being able to free themselves – an obsessional, occasionally modifying account of the same events. In dreams the same detail will occur in different narrative patterns: fragments of some intolerable idea. The patchwork-quilt effect of the Bible – texts by various authors, emendations, scrawlings over, discardable revisions that do not destroy the former text, contradictory, repetitious, often opaque re-thinkings – these are like the reasonings of someone awesomely shaken by the unbelievable nature of revelation.

The story of Adam and the story of Noah relive the same transforming, shock events. We do not know which of them was closest to the source.

The discovery of various clay tablets [in Mesopotamia] enables us to trace the Flood story back at least to 2000 BC . . . In the earliest tablets the Flood preceded the story of Paradise, which was occupied, not by the first man, but by the sole survivor of the deluge. This man ... was a gardener like Noah, and with a name equivalent to the Hebrew Noah. (Schofield, 1938, p. 40)

Drowned world

The Ark slips on a rocky edge; its doors swing open: Noah steps out into a new world. His eyes rest on lakes, rivers and watery skies, untarnished, unscratched, uninhabited by man, disease or death. The world might have never existed before this moment. He is like his ancestor, Adam.

Unlike Adam, he has a past. His past is an experience of everything having been wiped out. A whole world has drowned. In the Babylonian telling of the tale – under the name of Gilgamesh – Noah weeps over those who have died. In the *Epic of Gilgamesh*:

> The storm writhed like a woman in labour. On the seventh day the rain died down; the sea withdrew to its bed; the violent wind ceased. I looked on sea, at the same time shouting: but all mankind had returned to clay. I opened a window; and as the light fell upon my face, I shrank back weeping. On every side I looked on sea. (1972, p. 111)[1]

A time of annihilation. Only the Ark survives in this universal greyness. God had once divided the waters from the waters, dividing the waters which were under the firmament from the waters which were above the firmament 'and it was so'.

Thales, the Milesian, was to discover the world's unifying principle in water. God's beautiful geometric decision discovers an unexpected difference in this common element, seeing not the unity in difference, but the differences in unity, of water and water. The firmament, like a man-made cassone, or chest, or Ark floating in nothingness, contained a substance that is different, by the very nature of its containment, from the substance beneath.[2] The cistern that holds the rain makes rain different in some essential from the jets that rise up from beneath the ground – underground rivers, or mysterious subterranean sources (like Coleridge's Alph): springs, geysers, fountains. The distinction between the two waters is lost at the time of the great Flood. Rain lashes down as the seas rise up. Earth becomes a sponge, dissolving into its own exudations.

The Ark spirals through nothingness; it is buffeted by sourceless liquids. Tides stream through the abyss. The living, vernal, impulsive world, so careful in its nurturing categories, is shrunk into a space so restricted that sardonic Apelles, disciple of Marcion, thought that it could have held, at most, four elephants (Allen, 1949, p. 71). The flora and fauna and animals of the paradisal garden huddle skin to skin; extracts of their former selves, seeds to bridge the gap between generation and generation. The fragile and minute system of transmission, the semen blueprint out of which a universe emerges, is described as a covenant between God and man. If I forget the covenant – the rainbow in the cloud, guarantee of fertility and succession – I will find myself overwhelmed by the deluge.

All goodness and life-flow shrink into a tiny place. Badness swells up and floods the rest: chaos. The Ark outlasts a time of annihilation. It is one, among many, of the shelters in the Old Testament that resist oblivion: tabernacles or towers or Bionic exoskeletons, snail shells, more secure than tents, places of retreat from the whirl of creation and destruction, shrines and temples – interiors marking out holiness and learning (or profanity and dissipation). Nearly always, the sites are relatable to the transmission of fertility. Abstractions of places, anticipations of the hallowed monument – as in the area about the Bethel stone, where Jacob dreams of a ladder stretching up to the heavens. Or actual sky-aspiring structures like the Tower of Babel.

God's creation is absolute, so overwhelming in its authority, that we do not have the mental space to think of other possible worlds – of foetal existences that have not been granted life. Unavailable potentials did not haunt Adam – at least at first. Presumed to be satisfied by God and the universe, he was not thought to be potentially a malcontent.

Seemingly, he did not yearn for other possibilities. He was aware of an absence in possibility, though. God, sensing unhappiness, created Eve out of his body to fill the absence. Eve brings the idea of other possible worlds, and of imagination, into the present world: and with it, or so it is said, she brings the strange trio of death, disease and sin.

The perfection of absolute creation, of God's making in the first days, carries the Noah story as its shadow – the weeping and loss of an old world which, in time, most human beings have to suffer. Adam has no parents, no experience of sibling loss to mourn. The dimension of past and future, with its mourning possibilities, is introduced by Milton. And Milton allows Adam to dream of Eve. This is the same as to listen to parents telling stories and to be assisted by the tone of their voices – a modality unsuited to the sublimity of the Creation myths in Genesis.

Continuity

The Noah story describes the possibility of a thin thread of continuity: the 'something' that persists during a time of universal destruction or creation. The continuity is barely there – the extent of its being barely there cannot be overemphasized. At one moment the future of all living things depends upon the flutterings of a bird's wings.

The price to be paid, in terms of guilt and sorrow, may prove too harsh for the survivors. On one occasion at least, Noah was found drunk. Some commentators think that Noah was drunk because he was unaware of the power of wine. Noah took to drink perhaps because he found living with his memories of the Flood too painful to bear. He had to live with the thought that God's efficiency in destruction as well as in creation had not, as yet, included him among the dying.

If I can allow myself – if only temporally – to consider that the present moment contains absolute creation and absolute destruction – that the fact of the world puts a pressure on me so great and persistent that I need to ignore it in case its pressure annihilates me – then I will need the concept of continuity as some point of contact between absolute creation and absolute destruction. I become aware of how naïve I am, a foetal Adam; and how, in my naïvety, I may have to create the idea of continuity as a phantom link to which I can hold. It is the only way I can keep in mind the contradiction of absolute creation and absolute destruction.

The passionate desire men had to demonstrate their descent from Noah is only related in part to their need to believe in the Bible as a historical document. Being related to Noah, being able to believe in continuity through extreme vicissitude, allows me to experience the visionary metaphysical identification of absolute creation and absolute destruction, the essential content of the present moment. If something survives, then I can be born and die. If I can be born or die, I need some ground against which I can experience these vicissitudes.

The absolute vision confronts me at every moment, whether I grant it consciousness or not. It is the tale that needs neither teller nor listener, the eternal recurrence, the Freudian conflict between the unconscious life and death instincts, which is at the core of any set of beliefs I may have. I cannot wish the conflict away, nor would I want to, but I can add another dimension to it.

Man's mortality, his perishability, is the one sure thing he has. By inclination possessive, he must lose everything, including himself. He may experience the thought of his own perishability, the God of absolute destruction, as being like some dissociated entity inside himself, wreaking havoc – the bullet that pierces a tank's armour and spins around the interior killing everyone (as is the effect on Hamlet of his father's ghost). Or more benignly he may come to the experience of perishability through some self-transforming object within, the body of a duke imagined drowned though actually alive, a non-existent water-transformed body – a source of the imaginative in *The Tempest*. 'Those were pearls that were his eyes.' The idea of death, the God of absolute destruction, underlies such a person's idea of imaginative transformings; it may underlie all ideas of change.

How man experiences perishability as a prospect depends on how he understands the concept of legality, of the primal contract.

The drownings of Noah

God's covenant-making is essential to his creativity. Neither he nor his creatures can dissociate themselves from it. To be dissociated from it would be to lose any definition. The unceasing act of creation binds me to it, as though in law. The persistent and timeless re-creation of the whole universe in mythic thought contractually binds me to the pulse of renewal, whether I acknowledge its existence or not. The notion of law derives from the primal act of creation itself.

The world is absolutely before me, in the plenitude of every moment of perception. The world will be absolutely taken away from me in the moment of dying. The nature of human creativity – the forms of life within me – depends on how seriously I accept the covenant. If I fail to take it seriously, my prospects, already dim, will cease to exist. Well-being depends on my being allowed to be an agent for the future, to enjoy the nurturing function. If I am estranged from primal creation – the absolute power of *natura naturans* – if I find myself without the contract, if I recognize myself to be illegitimate, I will become powerless and I will drown.

For covenant-making implies covenant-breaking, as legality implies illegality or legitimacy implies illegitimacy. And yet, in recognizing this, I find myself wishing to rebel. I sense that the beautiful notion of the covenant has turned perverse. It has fallen into the hands of the self-righteous.

A great deal of social thought and ingenuity is devoted to making my neighbour into the illegitimate one: the one who has no rights, the one who is left out of the club, the one who is murdered at times of murder, the one who takes my place at the unwelcome moment of dying. The pressures of birthright or of deathright – of unequal acquirings and losses of talent as well as of possession – encourages the demarcations of legality and illegitimacy. Think of Abel and Cain, or Esau and Jacob.

Texts

Recalling the reading of passionate texts in adolescence – texts which over the years have continued to resonate in mind – creates an imaginary ancestral past that adds dimension to a past only scantily known. Enriching adolescence by losing myself in texts, often more deeply than in actual events, gave me an imaginary tenure in earlier times which otherwise I would not have had – a tenure more forming of self than many an actual experience.

My imaginative history, beginning in Genesis, came to an awesome stepping-stone in *King Lear*. I saw some kinship in Genesis and *King Lear*: here were origins of the questing generous self. In construing an imaginary history of this kind, I had a precedent in William Blake, who had passion's justification in believing that the British had descended from a lost tribe of Israel. Blake in turn drew precedence from Milton, who had covered certain chronological gaps in his *The History of Britain* by alluding to the Lear myth, as well as the legend concerning the coming to England of Noah's son Japheth.

Sceptically, Milton describes the unknown and unlikely sagas of Albion. Nothing is certain before the coming of Julius Caesar:

> . . . relations heertofore accounted fabulous have bin after found to contain in them many footsteps, and reliques of somthing true, as what we read in Poets of the Flood, and Giants little beleev'd, till undoubted witnesses taught us, that all was not fain'd. (Milton, 1971, p. 3)

The historian may discount the value of saga, but 'fables' are of use to the judicious poet.

The poet who looked to Genesis rather than to the legends of King Arthur as the subject matter for his epic presumably had some powerful impulse to bring together a belief in an actual King Lear with the belief that one of the tribes of Israel should have been among the first inhabitants of Britain. As a Puritan and an Englishman he feels much closer to the first parents than to Arthur. The garden of Eden for him (as well as for me) is in England now, and so is Fall, dispossession, exile and covenant. And so too is the belief that revelation is the primary vehicle of truth. Who am I? When I ask myself this question I will find that at my heart's core the wanderings of a dispossessed king near Dover and the migrations of dispossessed patriarchs take on the same crucial significance to my being.

Being interested in the nature of our first parents, and in questions of individual identity, encourages an interest in questions of a nation's origins. We cannot know about these events as historians; but the community can feel a pressure on it to create sagas; to this extent, the creation of sagas has the same inevitability about it as the creation of rumours.

> That the whole Earth was inhabited before the Flood, and to the utmost point of habitable ground, from those effectual words of God in the Creation, may be more than conjectur'd. Hence that this Iland also had her dwellers, her affairs, and perhaps her stories, eev'n in that old world those many hunderd years, with much reason we may inferr. After the Flood, and the dispersing of Nations, as they journey'd leasurely from the East, Gomer the eldest son of Japhet, and his off-spring, as by Authorities, Arguments, and affinitie of divers names is generally beleev'd, were the first that peopl'd all these west and Northern Climes . . .

Milton continues:

> A certain Samothes or Dis, a fowrth or sixt Son of Japhet, whom they make about 200 years after the Flood, to have planted with Colonies; first the Continent of Celtica, or Gaule, and next this Iland. (Milton, 1971, pp. 4–5)

95

In imagination, Lear wanders for ever by Dover.

Dispossession

Old, and about to die, Lear deludes himself into thinking he has a token future, the kingdom whose rights of succession he hopes to negotiate with his daughters. He wishes to raise himself in the face of an unavoidable fact, his own death – the Cordelia voice within and without the self that says, 'No' – by making a covenant with those who will succeed him. His covenant must fail, much as (in the Syriac *Book of the Rolls'* account of the Adam story) God's covenant had failed. God in failure must identify with the most helpless of his creatures in order to redeem Adam. He must become the infant Adam never was, suffer despair in death and progress through hell.[3]

Lear does not wish to suffer dispossession. But something like this fate is given him. As a prelude to the weaning of death, he must be weaned in life. He loses almost everything he loves in life before losing everything in death. He enters a deluge – Noah could have shaken hands with him. His hovel is barely an Ark, though, and he has no wish to preserve the human race. He prays for thunder to destroy all transmissions of seed – 'Crack nature's moulds, all germens spill at once' (*King Lear* III. ii. 8). Ostracized, made illegitimate, he finds himself, with Edgar and the Fool, put beyond the legal bounds of sense. They talk nonsense of various kinds. To those who wish to extend the bounds of legitimacy, they speak poetry.

The righteous person uses concepts of the madness, non-sense or good-sense kind to project painful states of illegitimacy into others and sees knowledge as a club to keep out non-scientific or nonsense-speaking brothers and sisters. But knowledge is more like the potential community of the disabled, a creative community at present scattered.

Suffering thoughts, enduring, being patient, becomes Lear's necessity. Opening himself to the impersonal powers of life and death within the self, he enters into a dangerous commitment.

I say with some irony that in order to survive, I seek to modify Lear's discovery in vocation. All thoughts, being potentially dangerous, have to be legitimized – to be made socially acceptable – in order to be defused. Otherwise, they may be rejected as nonsense. I test out the range of thoughts which I can tolerate in myself. I test out the thoughts which the society I live in will tolerate. A good deal of human activity, or intrigue, is devoted to negotiating with others the quota of acceptable thoughts.

Notes

1 The version of the passage quoted here is taken from King (1918, p. 82). Among certain peoples – the Winnebago Indians, the ancient Egyptians and the Khonds of Bengal, for instance – the tears wept by our first ancestors actually created the world.

2 The existence of the firmament is mentioned eight times in the first chapter of Genesis. It was apparently upheld on pillars. Von Rad, in his study of Genesis (1970), points out that the Hebrew word for firmament has some kinship to a verb used to refer to the beating out of metal. It was something made, a hammered-out metal structure – an indicating, if this were needed, that God the artificer was intent on architectural forms that would survive. For the primal God, even the inane azure is solid. Von Rad describes the firmament as a chastened metal dome. It had lattices to let the rain through.

3 Professor Northrop Frye investigates the likeness between Lear and the Old Testament patriarchs in his book, *Fearful Symmetry. A Study of William Blake.* He thinks that in one passage in the play at least – Lear's 'Upon such sacrifices, my Cordelia, The Gods themselves throw incense' – 'Old Testament allusions are piled up with a Blakean rapidity' (Frye, 1947, p. 373).

12

The literalism of God's word

TO READ Genesis in a way that allows it dimension, I need to read it literally, and not as a metaphor (or displacement) for something else. I cannot afford to start from the security of normative conceptions and see the text as some strange outcrop. The neurotic self is body-constrained, compelled by the issues of appetite, inclined to see any issue that is not appetite-compelling as a rationalization of appetite. Genesis, for the neurotic self, is a fanciful re-telling of the conflict between fellaheen and bedouin, the crop-grower and the shepherd. Hypersensitive to the frustration of his desires, the neurotic self assumes that everybody else, including the writers of Genesis, must suffer from his limitations.

But what if Genesis is the word of God, as the psychotic believes, irrefutable and unchangeable, allowing no place for the role of editor, a role which by its edgily perfectionist nature is neurotic? Not one jot or tittle can be changed of the original text – which turns out to have been written by the one author who is irrefutable – the author being nobody, and nobody cannot be denied. Genesis is a tale without a teller. And possibly without a protagonist. For its first cause – its possible teller or protagonist – does make himself manifest. He has characteristics to be sure, and these should be evident; but neither of his characteristics – of being absolutely creative and destructive, can be directly apprehended by man.

As someone converted to Genesis, I have difficulty in relating its ways of seeing to the world of naturalism, which I find dismally given over to issues of appetite. I am bewildered by the world's claims to be free-standing: claims that depend on the belief that the self can be separated to some extent from its environment. I am bewildered by the allusive and metaphoric manner of the world's communications; its pluralism; its innumerable agencies, each displacing energies and units of meaning among each other. As someone at home in the monism of Genesis, I do not understand the concepts of projection and hallucination. Nor do I understand the concept of sincerity, with the implicit importance it discovers in individual makings of truthfulness. I endorse Jeremiah's belief that only the false prophet speaks out of his heart. The true prophet allows God to lodge in his mouth, as though a mouth can be taken on lease. The true prophet denies his own individuality; he becomes God's voice.

I think if I were to visit the world from Genesis, as though from a foreign planet, I would find only one place that was not discomfiting; and that would be, for me (as well as for Adam), an imaginary place: my present conception of foetal life *in utero*. Genesis only finds its appropriate naturalistic reflection in post-birth reveries about the nature of pre-birth.

Genesis and pre-birth

Genesis 1–11 re-tells the same story, as though weaving the same piece of cloth or re-living again and again the processes of pregnancy. Each time the issue is different, and each time the process is roughly the same. There is an act of making. The act of making, and the time in the garden, are finite: even the inhabitants of the Ark must die. The tower, in breaking, allows the cradle to fall.

And yet there is something else, a continuous renewal – an absolute creativity beyond the understanding of fiction. A future existence pulses within some concealed place.

A pregnancy, a life, the writing of a book are acts of making that must come to an end. A plurality emerges. Things scatter: unity is lost. The newborn infant faces the blinding, conflicting interests of the obstetric ward. The dead person becomes a disintegrating corpse – also thoughts, and absences of thought, in the minds of survivors. The author of the completed book must face the mild disillusion of mind disengaged from theme.

This is how the Imagination happens to be; it allows us to experience a world as one and then a world in separation. Its biological origins lie in a pre-birth experience, which it attempts to retrieve. If I try to understand how the monistic conception of the Imagination has continued to exist in a pluralistic world – in which it is meaningful to speak of separation and otherness – then I must consider how once it was.

Presumably, the foetus has no reason to believe that it might be distinguishable from its environment – it does not experience its environment as an otherness available to scientific investigation. A foetus probably cannot differentiate its own skin from the skin of the maternal surrounding against which it rests. The maternal skin appears to wrinkle and fall away, like a loosened stage backdrop, at the time of parturition.

Theories of projection will have no place in experience before the differentiation of me and non-me – and Genesis exists in such an experience. Such theories imply some outwardness into which mind enters; separates of mind which can be intruded into: pluralities, in fact, which the foetus can have no knowledge of. Delusions and hallucinations are failures in experience which only someone who has been born, and someone who (in being born) has failed to experience birth, can be said to have.

Tiles

In states of psychopathology, I carry over into a later stage of development conditions of being which are appropriately sane at an earlier stage. All human thoughts and actions are good, if not denied their appropriate place. To interpret experiences of an earlier stage in terms of experiences of a later stage of development arouses a needless distress. To talk to a patient in terms of projections when the patient feels identified with a foetus, who knows nothing as yet of projection, would be an example of getting such a level wrong.

A man enters the grounds of the wrong house, when in fact hoping to turn up for his therapy session. He notices tiles on the path. He expects to see tiles on the path. The tiles he sees today are slightly different from the ones he usually sees. He realizes he has entered the wrong grounds: newly raised scaffolding nearby has misled him as to the position of the house.

It is possible that for a moment, deludedly, he did think that someone had rebuilt the entire street in order to deceive him. (A demon re-stages the world in order to torment me – a delusion of this kind would be characteristic of jealousy in the infant, who thinks its mother changes bodily in pregnancy in order to deceive him. She is not quite the same mother as the mother he knows and loves, and he views the slightest change in her with a tremor of suspicion.) A state of persecution of this kind was not unfamiliar to the patient. It did not do justice to the drastic nature of his experience. The jealous infant is not necessarily hand-in-glove with its environment. The patient was hand-in-glove. He needed the setting to be exactly right, as though it were a skin that was his skin. Deprived of rightness, he felt that all familiar contexts had been taken away from him; it was as though he had been ripped out of his skin.

The firm he works for had moved to a new address. A colleague (with whom he is identified) had taken a precious plant to the new office late one evening; and in the dark, and unable to find the light-switch (no longer in the same place), the colleague had fallen downstairs, and later had almost died from his injuries. It is as though one familiar place had been replaced by another, alien one: a context wrenched away, dissociating the colleague/patient from familiar places and calendars. A state in which the self is contained by a maternal skin as well as by its own skin is replaced by a state where the self has no confidence in its own single layer of skin. As this account suggests, extreme pre-birth anxieties probably underlie the more definable jealous anxieties of a sibling's birth.

I can read Coleridge's *The Ancient Mariner* as the inspired product of a psychopathology – its author being an addict poet, its narrator a guilty mariner. Or I can read it as though derived from an earlier stage in the psyche, as an imaginative or uterine experience, in which the concept of projection has no part. The seascapes through which the mariner travels are like a backdrop, or skin, which cannot be distinguished from the narrator's skin, an extension rather than a projection of his sensations.

The ancient mariner's world is as he sees it. He does not hallucinate it. The world he sees is in logic, the world that exists before the possible functions of hallucination have come into being. The nightmare settings that the mariner travels through exist on some poetic (or mental) map – as true in its way as any geographer's map. In a post-birth reading of the poem, I might imagine the albatross to be a good object, but one invaded by cynicism, and so transformed into a bad object that it blights nearly everything. Such a reading of the poem, and the uterine reading, do not exclude each other; the poem manages to be at the same time both decadent and true to the sane conception of the Imagination. In the same way, the foetus in its solitary sovereignty establishes its own norms, which if held to in the life after birth can become perversities.

Melanie Klein's observation that mind is capable of splitting off bits of itself and lodging them (often inextricably) in others depends on some recognition of plurality: on the fact that mind can no longer claim sovereignty over its support system. Klein believed that many of our problems would be diminished if pregnancies were by nature longer: we would tolerate plurality better.

The self that claims to be unable to differentiate me from non-me (because all evidences of me are physically woven into non-me), might argue that if the body has no boundaries – outward skin being confused with the uterine membrane – then mind will be suspended in a religious or imaginative atmosphere that will disappear at the rupturing of the atmosphere in birth, when an amphibian change occurs, a transition from water to air culture.

In his translations of Plotinus, A. H. Armstrong has Plotinus describe souls as 'amphibious' because they are compelled to live the 'life there and the life here,' either without or within the body (Plotinus, 1984, vol. iv, p. 411). Both Sir Thomas Browne and Coleridge use the term 'amphibious' to describe transitions between matter and spirit or between the figurative and abstract. The entry on 'amphibious' in *The Complete Oxford English Dictionary* cites Sir Thomas Browne's *Religio Medici*: 'We are only that amphibious piece between a corporall and spirituall essence' and Coleridge, who in *Biographia Literaria* speaks of 'An amphibious something . . . half of image and half of abstract meaning.' Meg Harris Williams has let me know that Browne uses 'amphibious' to evoke richness of association, while Coleridge uses it as an illustration of Fancy, Hieroglyphics and meaninglessness.

The capacity to think in terms of abstraction is relatable to the capacity to abstract spirit from matter, and in turn relatable to the ability of intelligence to move from one psychic environment to another.

13

The truest microcosm

ADAM'S ENVIRONMENT issues out of him. He is foetal and therefore unable to hallucinate. His warps, and the warps of the surrounding scene, cannot be distinguished. There is no question of anything being projected, since projection implies some otherness into which to cast the projection, and there is no otherness – in this, Adam is like the ancient mariner. The foetus discovers that the skin next to its skin is its own membrane. Foetal skin and its maternal surroundings are part of the same system – in the same way, the minds of God and Adam are indivisible.

Commenting on Sir Thomas Browne's *Religio Medici*, Coleridge asserts that 'the History of a man for the 9 months preceding his Birth would probably be far more interesting & contain events of greater moment than all the 3 score & 10 years that follow it' (Coleridge, 1981, p. 750). Browne had written, in the *Religio Medici*: 'every man is some monthes elder than hee bethinks him; for we live, move, have a being, and are subject to the actions of the elements, and the malice of diseases, in that other world, the truest Microcosme, the wombe of our mother' (Browne, 1643, p. 89; cited in Coleridge, 1981, p. 749).

'Live, move, have our being': the culture of the amniotic fluid is likened, as Coleridge was to liken the Imagination, to the sustaining atmosphere of the God, in whom (St Paul says) we live, move and have our being. The Pauline God gives human beings an atmosphere in which the Imagination can flourish, a uterine atmosphere which presumably God himself does not have use for.

The unborn self, thinks Browne, 'awaits the opportunity of objects; and seemes to live there but in its roote and soule of vegetation: entring afterwards upon the scene of the world, wee arise up and become another creature, performing the reasonable actions of man' (Browne, 1643, pp. 89–90).

The Genesis account of the world's creation is identical to the various stages of consciousness believed to evolve in the Aristotelian embryo, in which the creation of the plants precedes the making of the animals, which in turn precedes the ceremonial climax of the making of mankind. A vegetable foetus in a vegetable uterine world is transfigured into an animal foetus in an animal world.

This is an interesting way of thinking about the quality of the sympathy that I feel for every aspect of creation as (to use Browne's word) a 'compendium' – the way in which I feel interfused with other forms of organic life. But it does raise at least one question concerning the implicit issue of status in Creationism. Why should I presume to think of myself as more meaningful than a plant or animal, when I know so little about plants, animals or indeed myself? It seems that human beings have a great need to project a sense of inferiority and illegitimacy into others.

Transmigrations

In going to sleep, I put the experience of the Aristotelian foetus into reverse and find myself moving through animal states into the vegetative. The 'strange and mystical transmigrations' in uterus and chrysalis resemble the various changes in consciousness of someone who enters or leaves states of sleep: rites of passage in which I pass through states of death into apprehensions of a new life.[1]

The mythological imagination inclines to see such transmigrations as prompting belief in the immortality of the soul. Being born, being embodied, living out my life, is like the interregnum of sleep between two waking days.

> The smattering I have of the Philosophers Stone ... hath taught me a great deale of Divinity, and instructed my beliefe, how that immortal spirit, and incorruptable substance of my soule may lye obscure, and sleep awhile within this house of flesh. Those strange and mysticall transmigrations that I have observed in Silkworms, turn'd my Philosophy into Divinity. (Browne, 1643, p. 90; cited in Coleridge, 1981, p. 750)

There is in nature more than the 'eye of the common spectator' can discover. Nature is touched by a divinity which perplexes reason.

Coleridge refers, in both a letter and the *Marginalia*, to Browne's ability to discover unity in unlikeness: 'Whatever happens to be his subject, he metamorphoses all Nature into it.' As an example of Browne's splendour, he quotes (freely) from the celebrated final section of *The Garden of Cyrus*:

> ... the Quincunx of Heaven runs low, and 'tis time to close the five ports of knowledge; We are unwilling to spin out our awaking thoughts into the phantasmes of sleep, which often continueth praecogitations; making Cables of Cobwebbes and Wildernesses of handsome Groves ... there is little encouragement to dream of Paradise it self. Nor will the sweetest delight of Gardens afford much comfort in sleep; wherein the dulnesse of that sense shakes hands with delectable odours; and though in the Bed of *Cleopatra* can hardly with any delight raise up the ghost of a Rose ...

Though *Somnus* in *Homer* be sent to rowse up *Agamemnon*, I finde no such effects in the drowsy approaches of sleep. To keep our eyes open longer were but to act our *Antipodes*. The Huntsmen are up in *America*, and they are already past their first sleep in *Persia*. But who can be drowsie at that howr which freed us from everlasting sleep? or have slumbring thoughts at that time, when sleep it self must end, and some conjecture all shall wake again? (Browne, 1984, p. 387; quoted in Coleridge, 1981, p. 764)

The Imagination begins in pre-birth, and it declares the uterus to be the site of the authentic paradisal garden. By a reversal familiar to Platonists, it identifies sense experience with disembodiment – and reverie and dream with fallen man's recollection of a lost paradise. In the approaches of sleep, the self-transfiguring cosmos reveals itself as a series of meaningful coincidences: cobwebs become cables, the paradisal garden a ruined grove. The coincidence of the facts that the huntsmen should be up in America while other people are already past their first sleep in Persia – in the first instance an accidental conjunction – becomes, in reverie, a poetic making, in which the dreamer senses that the world is unified within his mind, as though he were still a foetus, while at the same time, outside him, as though in post-birth conditions, it would appear to spread out through tracts of space and time. Browne plays the languages of awakeness and those of reverie and sleep against each other. He rejoices in being the foetus at the centre, ordaining the nature of his surroundings.

Note

1 That transitions through symbolic states of death and rebirth universally underlie rites of passage is the contention of Arnold van Gennep (1960) in his impressive *Les Rites de passage* of 1908. Presumably to survive, the foetal self must move through autistic cycles of investment and divestment, simulations of birth and death.

14

Finding a focus

SEEING ONESELF at the centre of things in youth and early middle age can be pleasurable: the self as explorer, discoverer, intent on subduing and devouring all experience. But such a picture, though true of uterine conjecture, as I like to imagine it, is misleading. Buccaneer appetites give only a buccaneer view of things, centring all unknowability on the devouring self and its unceasing appetite. Egotism is like a medieval map. It begins with the confident areas of knowledge and moves out into blank spaces, a misleading depiction.

Years ago, I asked W. R. Bion in a public meeting if he agreed with Keats's view that a man's life of any worth might be a continual allegory. Characteristically, Bion answered the question in a way that made me wonder whether he had heard it. Life, he thought, was more like an alphabet: its components create a never-ending constellation of meanings. I am not sure I understand what either of us meant by this exchange.[1] Trying to understand was one of the starting points to this book, though one I have been glad to lose while in the writing. I have come to the view that any theory of meaning which posits self-consciousness as its centre does an injustice to the powers that mind can recognize. The insights of Genesis are not available to egocentric thought.

A patient in psychoanalysis one day recalled an abridged child's edition of Bunyan's *The Pilgrim's Progress*, which he had read when aged about ten. He thought the analysis had entered the doldrums. All initiative within him, if not in the analyst, lay with the forces of inertia. He thought of Bunyan's Slough of Despond: here he seemed to be sunk, and here it seemed likely he would forever remain.[2]

The Slough analogy gave the depression a provisional staging. The patient needed to find some equivalent to Keats's belief in living as having its allegorical aspect – whatever that might mean. Later the patient became persecuted. He felt trapped by the metaphor. He found the puritan ethos barbaric and incompatible with the self he wanted to be. And yet, at the same time, it was he who had spontaneously thought of the Bunyan analogy.

Unable to tolerate some disturbing conflict in feeling in himself, he had entered a condition of inertness, reached out for a metaphor, and imagined himself in Bunyan's Slough of Despond. I suspect that he had deceived himself – for the coming into being of the feeling is unlikely to precede the coming into being of the place. The place is always there; it precedes him; and he discovers it. In Genesis the place is always specific. God does not appear here and there. God is not an appendage to my states of mind, like the metaphoric Slough of Despond.

The grammar of Keats's 'A Man's life of any worth is a continual allegory' implies that an allegory is something a man of worth inherits or acquires. The intransitive nature of the sentence may stir wonder in the speaker. An allegory of what? Surely not the allegory of something; rather the other way round – since the something (which is unknowable) manifests itself through us, as though we were its allegory.

A Man's life of any worth is a continual allegory – and very few eyes can see the Mystery of his life – a life like the scriptures, figurative – which such people can no more make out than they can the hebrew Bible. Lord Byron cuts a figure – but he is not figurative – Shakspeare [sic] led a life of Allegory: his works are the comments on it. (Forman, 1935, pp. 303–4)

Unknown events, of immense power, write out our lives as though we were Shakespearean texts. The fact that each of us is a variation on an enigmatic theme is token of our brotherhood. The theme may exist on a different time-scale from ours. It may take centuries, or millennia, to be expressed; or it may exist outside time altogether. In the case of Coleridge, for instance, the Shakespeare experience offers, in microcosm, an experience of the whole world.

Keats moves from a picture of life as a journey, in the sense of migrations through material need, through the idea of migrations through spiritual need, into a picture of life as the text of an unknown and unknowable author. How do we understand the text if we do not know anything about its author? How, in fact, do we come to know anything about Genesis, say, or *King Lear*? We know nothing about the author(s) of the Old Testament and little about Shakespeare. Suppose God or Shakespeare had never existed: or the world as text had come into being without an author. Would this be like Bion's view of life as alphabetical, mysterious in the ways in which it forms into units of meaning?

The limitation of allegory – its being a fanciful device – is that it does not allow enough imaginative vigour to the idea of the unknown. Allegory, as an agnostic conception of the understanding, supposes that the idea as power, the all-powerful Platonic conception of idea, is no more than a manner of speaking, a convention useful in furthering discourse but with no authority in itself. The God of allegory is rationalization, abstraction, attentuation, shadow. This is a 'neurotic' conception of the idea. Keats admits to his distrust of intermittency and literalism in his allegory letter – both attributes being essential to psychotic intuition. A psychotic understanding of the idea (a Genesis understanding of God's overwhelming omnipotence) takes us closer to the idea's nature.

The allegorical Byron, like saint or hero, defines something in the culture. To cut a figure is to cut a dash: the emphasis is on outwardness, shaping, style as calligraphy, a poignant transience. The true life of allegory – Shakespeare's life – is largely unknown to us; it might not have existed; it might be unavailable to conscious thought. On the grounds of common sense, Shakespeare's works indicate a human authorship. Whatever it is that fills the content of the concept 'Shakespeare' is beyond the imagination of most of us. In this sense, the life of allegory is the life of the often hidden communicant who speaks to the people in the desert: revelation itself. Properly the people in the desert must imagine themselves to be the elements out of which the allegory is made, not its meaning. They are the letters of the alphabet, in themselves waiting for the arrival of meaning through acts of conjunction. Meaning originates in the unknowable – call the unknowable, if you wish, God. A man of worth will realize that the allegory of his life is not about himself but about something other: his life is the means by which an unknown event (or series of events) lives out its choice of meanings.

The mystery of things

The notion of life as a continual allegory is syntactically odd. We want to ask: where is the end of the sentence – what is it an allegory of? If allegory is a fixed element, a knowable quality, then I doubt the truth of the assertion. If the allegory points to a mystery, then it makes some sense: we 'take upon's the mystery of things as if we were God's spies.'

It might be argued with some plausibility that Shakespeare's plays, like dreams, defend the spectator against some intolerable unknown. They can intimate vision; whereas allegory can often mark the spot where a vision has been murdered. Or am I being unfair to the process of allegory? It is as though life came into being in body sensation and yearned to be something else; and decided to be this something else through an allegorical efflorescence.

Continuing city

The writer of the Epistle to the Hebrews, a follower of St Paul, describes how the strangers and pilgrims on earth seek a better country. No return to the paradisal garden, the horticultural paradise of the tillers of the ground, but a move forward to the beautiful 'continuing' city. 'For here we have no continuing city, but seek one to come' (Hebrews 13:14). John Keats also refers to the continual. The allegory of a man's life of any worth is 'continual'. It is, in its continuity, opposed to the literalism which Keats sees as 'shallow'. Keats is a man of the Ark in his desire for the continual. Perhaps human bondage to the metaphor of life as a journey has to do with our Noah-fears of being drowned, of dying from a condition of literalism and intermittency.

It would be misguided to assume that our lives are terrains that can be mapped out from the self as centre. Introspection as a pilgrimage of this sort can lead to allegorical narratives – and other forms of self-dramatization – but has a way of increasing isolation and egocentricity. The self (and not something other than the self) is believed to be the source for the generation of meanings: a seductive belief that increases love of the self and its powers. Bunyan's pilgrimage, Keats's belief in the good life as a continual allegory, Henry James's concern with the possibilities of the governing consciousness, indeed most forms of puritan investigation, tend to centre on a hero and his psychic furnishings; irresistible that the hero should be me, snug in the library-Ark of my mind, unable to hear the cries of the drowning.

Man is no more the measure of all things than is (thought Socrates) the dog-faced baboon. I do not live out my life: it lives me out; and this 'it' is the subject of any allegory of value.

Allegory takes on splendour if the allegorizer is God, not man; and the lives of men reflect or dimly apprehend the God-allegory, a tale without an apparent teller or listener. Tales with tellers, tales with listeners, are tales suspended in consciousness, subtly endorsing self-importance – books and family anecdotes furnish myths that enrich the sense of selfhood. Imaginary history begins in self-centredness.

Augustinian (Protestant, Puritan) sources in English culture assert that truth can be discovered through self-examination. The questing soul hopes to reach the Holy Spirit through introspection. To this extent, self-examination is a departure point in pilgrimage. But the nuances and structures of consciousness become loved for their own sake. I lose sight of the idea that consciousness is a possible vehicle for the Holy Spirit. The Puritan enterprise, by its centring on the nature of the individual conscience, leads to wonder at the wondrousness of consciousness. Notions of a pilgrimage give way to a self-admiring aestheticism. Having sensibility is the one thing that matters; there is no sense that qualities of mind contribute to anything but themselves.

At times, I feel dread at the thought of dying. I fear the annihilation of my consciousness. I forget that I have begun to learn the meaning of seriousness through having experienced the death and birth of others – of having borne witness to ineffable events – that I have begun to know the pre-Freudian ego D. H. Lawrence wrote about in the summer of 1914, an ego 'according to whose action the individual is unrecognisable.'

At the same time, I think my consciousness supremely important. Working it up, culturing it, has been a massive investment – like building an Ark in gopher-wood. I do not allow the fact that others value their own consciousness higher than I do mine to press in on me. My love for my consciousness and my high estimation of it are among my most treasured secrets. And the culture I live in encourages me to continue to polish and texture and enrich it. This is what much education is about, I fear – the development of sensibility, a nation of Ark-lovers, each of us enshrined perpetually in our Arks.

Notes

1 I think of a patient's association to a dream in which the lovely variety of colours in a child's paintbox was likened to the creative possibilities of the uterus: the walls of the box had the magical power to individuate life (through suffusion?). Perhaps in unconscious phantasy the letters of the alphabet function in the same way as the patient thought the colours in the box did.

2 The patient was sunk into torpidities of the soul and drawn towards particularities (an indication, in Plotinus, of the soul being drawn towards evil!). He was reasonably seeking some sort of self-definition through the uses of allegory. I am aware of how people in therapy, who feel impatient because some aspect of themselves is as yet unfocused, can reach out for allegory as they might reach out for a fact. If you feel all over the place, you need a map.

A woman in her first session with me keeps interjecting thoughts about dying, multiple sclerosis, calcifications of the bone. I am conscious of how difficult it is to tune into her and I wonder whether her interjections describe some sense she has of falling out of my consciousness. I begin to feel panic.

In the next session she tells me something that – when worked on – encourages us both. She had formerly been in group analysis. There had been a change in the meeting place. She and another member of the group, a male, had decided to drive to the new place together: she had driven the car, and he had guided her by reading the map. She was not too sure of her sense of direction, he had had trouble map-reading, and they had made mistakes – taking wrong turnings and so on – but eventually, with some sense of achievement, had reached the meeting place twenty minutes late. She had then experienced the leader of the group and some of its members as punitively turning on her companion and herself as a couple, accusing them of bad motives in their lateness.

I thought she was telling me that she could believe that a mother–baby relationship need not be idealized; since only an ideal mother has the capacity to be in tune with her baby at all times. (The patient had been rejected by her mother at birth and brought up in adoption. She tended to hold on to an idealized image of the perfect mother she had never had.) Admittedly the car-driver and the map-reader make a confused representation of the mother–baby couple – both of them have features suitable to the mother, neither of them is really the baby – but at least there is the idea of a couple working together. (I think the censorious therapy group represents aspects of herself that are hostile to the emergence of both good will and the acknowledgement of fallibility, qualities essential to the working together of any human couple.)

From the point of view of allegory, the interesting point is the idea that a receptivity in intuition in the couple should be thought of in terms of a map or a psychic topography. The map is a two-dimensional object, a text made up of signs, and in this sense is an inadequate representation of life in the mind, but provisionally it is immensely valuable in giving the couple a notation which allows it fullness of symbol creation (arrived at through receptivity), an activity which is their goal.

Thinking about this patient reminded me of another patient whose first months in therapy had been such an attack on the idea of hope and development that I had thought his aim in coming into therapy was to have me share with him the immediate prospect of his dying. His doubts about being tuned into by anyone were relatable to his hatred of the fact that some people, his parents as a couple especially, have a certain solidity of being. Their reality as existents in a certain space and time cannot be obliterated. He wanted to show me up as foolishly omnipotent in thinking he might be able to live (like the couple). Any evidence of optimism had to be disintegrated.

One day he brought a dream which was unequivocal in its meaning. He was travelling to a certain place, but took a round-about way through villages whose names crudely alluded to acts of self-mutilation. Eventually he reached a place by a river where two women asked for his help but he felt unable to be of use to them. I pointed out how allegorical this dream was, a *Pilgrim's Progress* (disabling a father, who is also his mother's lover, by disabling himself). He spat out this idea in a rage. He detested the allegorical way of looking at things.

It was clear that he did not want maps of the spirit of any kind, since such maps provide spiritual facts that challenge the wish to betray the good or to contaminate it with badness.

Uses of allegory mark a provisional but important stage in the development of trust and receptivity in the couple, baby and mother, the self and its objects. Sign language can usefully precede the act of symbol-making through a shared emotionality, though sign-thinking – the viewing of experience as text or allegory – is a labile process, easily liable to regress into the self-enclosing or autistic Ark of egotism.

15

The grove of Holy Writ

*How dreadful is this place! this is none other
but the house of God, and this is the gate of
heaven.*

Genesis 28:17

FOR BOOKISH men, the shrine at which they rest
might be within a book. Milton toyed with the
idea of an Arthuriad; it remained unrealized. Discovering
how the book of Genesis lay at the core of his emotional
being – at the core where the unknowable can transform into
meaning – he lay down in the grove of Holy Writ, and dreamt
Paradise Lost. You struggle to achieve allegory and you fail.
Art, like life, makes, then breaks you, lives you out and then
frees you into death. Adam does not create God in his own
image – God, the unknowable, creates Adam.

The 'major thing' about *Paradise Lost*, according to William Empson, 'is the fascination of its barbaric power.' He
compared it to 'appalling' African sculptures – bronze
masterpieces from the looted city of Benin – which 'raised my
spirits no end' (1961, p. 276). To a lesser extent than George
Fox perhaps, Milton was taken over by Holy Writ, as though
it were a holy place that determined dreams. Text acts him
out, shapes his body, gesturing cosmic lunges, upward
sweeps, sheer falls. The cosmos, and the very initial moment

of time, are his introspective sites. He needed absolutely the whole universe and the very beginnings of time to reach to the heart's core.

Empson sensed something dreadful in mind and certain art, and he thought this something had a Christian source. Unknowable ideas often take unwelcome forms; they manifest themselves disgustingly. Any decent person would shrink from having something so horrible as a mind. But perhaps only a genuinely decent person would admit to having a mind – indecent people tend to mindlessness, to act out their indecencies rather than to admit to them; they wish to disown mind. The question of likeability or desirability is beside the point. I suppose that Milton's God was a *natura naturans* or creative element in Empson that Empson could hardly bear.

Ancestor voices, loved voices of the lost ones, speaking intimately about lost things, personalized experiences, stories in which the tellers give conflicting accounts of the same tale, babbling – these take us away from the unitary vision which exists outside death and loss. They can also turn very bad, becoming the devil within the man-made image, that impels the living to sacrifice their children. Our ancestors can horribly manufacture us in ways that are unlike the makings of God. They speak to us in the swollen, dropsical distended faces of African sculpture, faces possessed by a living pastness – speaking to you and me, their presently-living about-to-be sacrificed children. Envying aliveness, the dead can seem to hate the living for having temporarily survived the Flood. They point out the way, grimly; they know that even Noah must drown in time.

Beliefs of this kind are the source of paralysing illness. In Augustine's view, Adam and Eve continue to live in the present – as parasites living out our host lives. The sin of the primal parents poisons every subsequent generation of mankind. Its toxicity intensifies with the passing of each generation. Or at least this is one scenario among the theories of introspection.[1]

Fluke

Paradise Lost is a fluke in place and time, unusual in any understanding of how the puritan comes to meaning. Barbaric qualities, the tribal past, in Milton's inner world speak out, unforgivably. A poet, made by his work of art, finds himself unable to escape a rising substrate of images and places and journeyings within the self that have always been there. I come to know what I have always (perhaps) known. I come to face something (often terrible) that breaks and makes me. This can happen in psychoanalysis. I meet myself, this passionate and horrible layer in self that I wish to disown but which is me, the matter of art, mind itself, that which I want reasonably to destroy. A work of art is a Platonic idea of immense power that uses its servant, the artist, and then discards him, having realized itself through him.

If Adam were to make God in his own (idealized) image, his God would be lifeless, an illusion, in the sense that some people talk of art as 'illusion' – or allegory as a picture-book illustration to their lives. Such a God would be God in a manner of speaking, a convention (like zero in mathematics), not an articulating, disturbed power. Such a God would not be able to talk to us, as God spoke to Adam. Such a God would not be the primal creation.

Rather, as Genesis says, God makes Adam in his own image. I do not make something, if the something is of psychic importance: it makes me. Allegory only takes on power as a literary device if I think of the unknown as allegorizing my life – myself being the allegorized entity that represents something else.

Possessed by Adam

Some people are overwhelmed by their being of the class of Adam: they feel possessed by Adam. They are unable to see the facts. There is a joy so overwhelming that it seeks to take everything into it; it discounts the otherness of otherness.

The idea is no longer situated at some distance from me. It has moved in so close that it has taken me over. Adam and

Eve are me, and they live out my life. When a Blakeian walks through present-day London he is put in mind of Bibleland. It occurs to him that Bibleland is the true place; present-day London, a veil to the truth. Without Bibleland, as the generator of meaning, the contemporary London of Blake makes no sense.

For Blake, the Old Testament is not analogy. It is the present world that is analogy to the Old Testament. In entering into a dialogue with the unknown God, he comes to recognize himself as a member of the Adam class. Imaginary history nourishes the heart.

If all history is about God and man, then I have the choice of identifying either with God or man. If I identify with God – if I treasure my own consciousness as the primal source of creativity – then I will find myself identified with a unique entity; but my self-centredness will be exposed in its creative incapacity. If I identify with man, then logically I identify with all mankind, my experience being a variant on the experience of Adam.

Unknowabilities, neither conscious nor unconscious, determine our lives. I have intimations of these events through their effects. The wreckage after a storm, the change in the contours of a stone beach after a tide, the resonance of music or places often imply the directly unknown idea. Some people are gutted. They intimate a former undamaged self: an exceptional ability – to be able to sense the power of the good – is matched by states of an extreme intolerance to the good. People of this kind are tormented, swept about, possessed by *natura naturans* – an unknowable idea in the process of destroying them. For them, there need be no devil and no wickedness; the good is deluvial, devil-work. They sense the goodness of the world as an unceasing torment; it works on them as though it were an evil.

A woman felt herself under attack from violent sexual images. She arranged her life so that she was frequently faced by brutal scenes – cut throats, needles stuck into veins, and so on. She fuelled herself with emblems of violent conjunction.

It turned out that these were transformations in her mind of a loving relationship whose ineffability she could not bear.

Menses

When I think of witchcraft, I think: this is how some of my patients experience life during the times when in a session they explore manifestations of their unconscious. Being in touch with this dimension seems to be important to psychic health. Mind needs to retrieve its passionate, complicated, occult dimension. (Similarly, the art of Africa, often described as 'primitive', has been a primary source of inspiration in this century: it has revolutionized the practice and idea of art.)

A woman dreams that she is with her mother, who is comatose and possibly dying. Someone else is there, who accuses her of lateness and so on. She cannot bear the accusations. She takes hold of the hands of her accuser and twists back the fingers.

The accuser reminds her of her cousin Betty. When she was aged fifteen, she came home to her aunt's house one evening and found Betty sitting there, dressed in a red dressing-gown and drumming her fingers on a chair-arm. Betty accused her of causing her aunt much distress by her lateness. The aunt happened to be in bed upstairs, and it turned out that she was not distressed; she was surprised by Betty's claim to authority.

About the red dressing-gown – I ask, has it anything to do with menses? She tells me that she feels heavy from a bad period and sore nipples. She has long had these problems – and so has Betty. Her mother used to proudly boast that she had never had problems with her periods from beginning to end. Good reason, I presumed, for her being triumphant over a dying mother – as though she had believed her mother a witch who had put torment into Betty and herself. They would writhe on the floor clutching hot-water bottles.

You think to have the experience; it thinks to have you; it swells up and possesses you. In certain African masks, faces distend as though in a terminal agony: ancestor-possessed. Discovering the Holy Spirit within is not necessarily an agreeable or commendable experience.

What I am trying to do is to sort out the good from the bad in the theory of being projected into. Is being possessed by the unknown God the same as being possessed or projected into by witches or envious ancestors? Potencies in the mind cannot be kept in compartments. They necessarily move about and do what they like. If I try to lock them away, I am liable to lock myself into nullity.

Something moves about in my mind; I do not know what this thing is. Its modes of symbolization – its way of making itself manifest to me – may be disgusting. It may manifest itself to me in the form of intolerable obsessional thoughts that make me loathe the fact that I have a mind.

Grandfathers

A child talks about her grandfathers as though she knew them – makes up stories about them; gives them the same name, Peter. When she talks in this way, I do not think she is talking about my father and my father-in-law, who were her actual grandfathers. I think she is talking to me as though I were a reflection of herself and the grandfathers she is talking about are my grandfathers also. She wants me to share her mythology: I might be her twin brother. Grandfathers and fathers are agents in her mind for something else. She is mythologizing about a painful experience of having a loved father she cannot possess, possibly trying to make the experience tolerable to live with. She deals with the pain of being father-possessed by being father-inspired. Is her condition the same as someone's who thinks she is being projected into by witches?

When I had seen her make her drawings I had asked myself: does the inspiration come from within or without? Where does the icon come from? In a certain sense, neither from within nor without. The marks on the paper appear as a dream appears in sleep. A dream takes us over and insists on bearing witness in the world. I cannot be sure what it bears witness to; I would like to forget it but cannot – and I would like to think it motivated by some unreasonable disturbance.

A child can make pictures in the same way as dreams can manifest themselves to the adult. Mind extemporizes around an intolerability, as the oyster extemporizes a pearl. Presumably the oyster does not think itself author of the pearl. Hard to believe in the concept of authorship: no trouble in believing in the grit that irritates the oyster.

Does God make Adam in the same way as the child makes its painting? Was God as Adam-possessed as Adam was Eve-possessed?

Note

1 For a dependence on persecutory internal objects, see Lévy-Bruhl:

> Nothing tells [primitive men] that they would be interested in trying to find out about the laws governing natural phenomena; they have no conception of it. What attracts their attention . . . is the presence of invisible powers . . . For their protection and defence against these they have the traditions transmitted by their ancestors and their confidence in these appears unassailable. (Lévy-Bruhl, 1936, p. 20)

16

A moderating concerned presence

I HAVE an experience which allows me to see how shallow my feelings had been. For instance, I meet with the experience of birth or death for the first time. I think to find myself in touch with Lawrence's 'ego according to whose action the individual is unrecognisable.' I had not thought a seriousness of such depth existed. It puts me in touch with states of being I would deny, of my having a soul, a vulnerable foetus within the infant self, alert to the fluctuations of life and death.

A presence within me has become suffused by the deeper powers of absolute creation and destruction. At times the presence is terrifying; it comes close and seems to take me over. Alternatively, I may feel it keeps its distance in order to protect me, to enable me, to moderate terror.

A man dreams that he is in a theatre or cinema. Someone – situated high up behind him – asks: where do you want me to direct the light beam? He answers playfully: up left.

He gave associations to the dream. Most of them related to

his wish to be the family star actor who directs the beam of a father's attention.

One of the associations, of a different calibre, half-buried, almost escaped notice. It took the form of an image. His father was poring over an X-ray negative placed against a luminous screen. (His father had been long dead.) The dreamer mentioned the image and then pulled away from the idea in a way that prompted me to pause over it.

He recalled how, in mid-puberty, he had contracted tuberculosis – he had been kept in a state of convalescence for over a year. He had declined to take his illness seriously. He had found reasons for not taking it seriously. He had thought obscurely that it was a form of punishment; he felt guilty about being away from school; he was already aware of his pleasure in hypochondriasis; and so on. All these thoughts were ways of directing the beam of attention on to himself, so that he would be the star of a show which his parental audience would have to look at, if only with disapproval. He thought he did not know any other way to interest it.

The image of his father looking at the X-ray shadow on his lungs, once acknowledged, changed the meaning of the dream. His father, a doctor, had been concerned about his illness with a seriousness of concern beyond the dreamer's powers. The stage on which the dreamer found himself was quite different from the entertainment theatre he had imagined – it was more like an operating theatre. His father had known that his child was at risk; had loved him, and treasured the preciousness of his life – in a way that was beyond the child's conscious understanding. The patient, becoming an adult, had continued to deny that he was genuinely at risk.

In loving the child, in allowing himself to feel some anxiety at its welfare, the father was responding to some essential preciousness in the child, whose existence had to be fought for. The father was in touch with the child's soul, the foetus within the infant, forever in the process of undergoing birth, of enduring the creative act of labour, of suffering the creativity of others – its mother's creativity especially. Of its nature, the foetus within the infant forever exists on the borderline between life and death. Its life depends on tenuities: an olive branch in a dove's beak; the breath of God in Adam's mouth.

The dreamer had lodged in his father a capacity to think with a depth in feeling – and he did not think that this kind of thinking would be ever available to him. He felt reproached by the image of his father. He felt shallow by comparison; and he was reluctant to move out of the shallows. He was only able to experience a deepening of thought if he allowed himself to meet beloved presences in his mind who tolerated conditions of depth for him. Such meetings were necessarily poignant and shaming; and he could not stand them.

The image of his father poring over another image, the X-ray negative, was like a gift. Over the decades, the gift had been within his preconscious mind, awaiting discovery, as though in a kind of pregnancy; an Adam pulsing unobserved at the centre of the universe. Or a prohibited image that guiltily invited sacrifice.

He might have died without ever having discovered the gift. He was dissociated from the part of himself, lodged in the image of his father, which was capable of valuing the infant in himself. A presence within him carried his possible maturity. Only by meeting the presence in his mind, without the compulsive need to direct the beam of attention, could he become endowed with qualities that he at present feared in others.

He was genuinely moved by the session and grateful. Its short-term effect was to bring out his delinquency. It became clear that he confused feelings of helplessness with a tendency to fraudulence – and to mobilize one was to mobilize the other. He could not allow himself to be in touch with a father who feels passion for his child's helplessness – who perceives fraudulence and, in the face of the child's suffering, puts the fraudulence aside, at least temporarily, as a secondary matter. The image went bad within him.

It persecuted him and he behaved in a persecuted fashion.

In part, he could not suffer his pubertal illness because he could not suffer the meaning of his delinquency. His psychopathology now came to the fore. He dreamt that he was murdering the therapist. The formerly diffused delinquent traits in his behaviour took on a sharply delineated configuration, as though on an X-ray negative. He began to fall to bits. Thoughts concerning his father's loving care for him activated the fear – always there, beneath the surface – that his mother would be pregnant once more. (He had been the youngest child.) His car broke down in a busy London street. He was attacked by panic. The coil in the car, he said, had not been working. He had directed the light beam in himself with one intention only, to mislead the creativity in others. He had used the light beam contraceptively, as though it were a coil that hinders procreation.

In subsequent sessions, he was frequently to refer to broken-down vehicles of one kind or another. The meaning of these vehicles was ambiguous: sometimes they referred to his sense of an impending breakdown, sometimes to a breakdown that he felt was mine. He wanted us both to feel that our relationship was in jeopardy. He was the infant at the breast who interprets its mother's pregnancy as a 'breakdown'. He was also identified with the foetus within the mother, projecting himself forward in time, into the younger sibling or the next patient, who would some day take his place. As the foetus, he sensed a similarity and sharing of body experience between himself and his mother – of being a couple who mutually face the threat to life of the birth labour: anxieties that the child who has been born tends to re-experience in less clear ways. If the mother's insides deteriorate, the foetus will probably die; if the foetus deteriorates, the mother's procreative system will probably go wrong. And if the foetus miscarries, the mother will probably break down. The broken-down car applies equally well to the condition of them both.

The concept of experience

The concept of experience is elusive, in part because it covers so many levels of immaturity in perception. The young adult in me may think that I 'have experiences' – it may see life as a series of conquests. The foetus within me will see things with a wisdom that the young adult has probably lost touch with, and which it may only regain after some submission to the act of death-and-birth known as the mid-life crisis. The foetus may see its great journey of birth as an undergoing: as something that must be undertaken, a continuous and necessary manner of breakdown. It does not have the experience; rather, in the manner of the Genesis Adam, the experience has it. Later it will think of experience differently – as a kind of ingestion, something to take in or have. In birth, though, an earlier, more suffering self will think of creativity as something to be endured: God's contract.

Saying that I 'have' an experience is like saying that the life of a man of worth is a continual allegory. It is to see the experience, and the allegory, as adjuncts to the self, like awards for bravery. An allegory of what, though? Of a mystery. But the mystery of its nature cannot be given the typology of an allegorical journey. Mysteries cannot be so described. Clearly, I have got it wrong. The allegory is not an adjunct, like my 'goodness' or my priestly robes, or the establishment newspaper I carry beneath my arm. I am merely an adjunct or vehicle to it. The mystery moves through me, whether I am aware of it or not. It is the mystery that travels, whose existence is the journey, taking me in its stride.

I do not make experience; experiences make me. The mystery would use me as the vehicle of a journey whose direction and point of arrival I have no way of knowing. I find that I want to include in any definition of experience the notion of a presence within me that embodies dimensions in feeling that I cannot tolerate – a someone or something that contains aptitudes and potentialities that may be buried from me, and that is contemplative in ways that my conscious self will possibly never benefit from. The father who pores over the X-rays of my mortal psychological disease – who senses the moment of possible dying in every moment of life – is able to consider the nature of life and death with a seriousness beyond my present grasp. Only perhaps when I come to observe the birth or death of others do I approach this sense of necessary awe.

The setting in the dream of the man who directs the light beam – either a theatre or cinema – is a fitting place for the expression in sound and movement of a certain range of experience: a suitable dream symbol for one among the many means by which human beings articulate themselves. The dream does not acknowledge the imaginative possibilities by which theatre and cinema can become vehicles for art. They are not seen as places that give expression to an otherness which is mysterious – a religious mystery being the necessary motive of art.

By implication, the dreamer sees himself as the director of the show, a God figure. The electrician who moves the beam of light to suit his vanity is presumably his father – a father who panders to a little boy's whims. Is there a mother in all this? Presumably she exists in the atmosphere of the mute or disabled creative site: a mother as place, the cinema or theatre chained to the dreamer's vanity.

Compare the beam of light with the diffuse screen light that shines through the X-ray negative, enabling the father to read the shadow on his child's lungs. The beam of light, in its sharp focus and extent of deployment, is too limiting a factor in any definition of experience. It reduces the meanings of experience to attention-directed thoughts or narrow modes of perception, perhaps like the Lockeian penetration of the self by impressions that register their presence – with some sharp quill-like point, surely – on blank surfaces. Such an acute object entering me, turns into some bad internality that cuts me into pieces from within.

But that which enters and lives within me need not be violent or sharp. Plotinus, comparing the Beautiful and the

Good, thought that the Beautiful was often lacerating. But the Good did not have this effect on him. The Good, he thought, was modest, unassuming and continuous, whether we recognize its presence or not. The existence of the Good implies mental possibilities which are seldom, if ever, available to conscious review – the realm of the unconscious in other words. (Plotinus invoked the concept of the unconscious in an attempt to account for the nature of the good, not the bad, in the self.)

Perhaps the issue of how an experience enters us is incidental to the possibility that some essential generative element in the experience has always been there. The beam of light becomes transfigured into a diffuse source of light that glows through an X-ray negative. Intelligence, like light, may distend over a wide surface: the diffused light source reveals some truth concerning the state of the child's lungs.

Good presences in the mind do not push me in this direction or that. Goodness is not obtrusive. It does not prey on my attention – I might live through a life without noticing it. If I attempt to manipulate the Good, it distances itself from me. The Good does not punish me for my ruthlessness to it; it avoids the beam of my attention; it seems to disappear; and with it the Imagination disappears also.

The father's looking at the X-ray is both scientific in motive (being a non-sensuous apprehension of the world) and religious (in the awe and urgency with which it contemplates the mystery of the illness). I would compare the beautiful thought of the father's looking into the X-ray negative, oceanic against its light, each transforming the other into a steadily deepening image of the power of perception, with Shakespeare's use of the ocean as symbol in *The Tempest*. The corpse of the Duke of Milan, Ferdinand's father, makes no demands on his son. The corpse just is – in a condition of magical self-transfiguration. It exists beneath water, in the watery depths of the imagination, in a culture different from the island air which the son inhabits. The corpse does not exist, in fact: the Duke is still alive. There is no body except in thought; the corpse being a figment of Ariel's imagination. Like Adam pulsing at the centre of the earth, its acts of self-transfiguration are purely imaginative.

The body of the Duke beneath water is a non-being, a symbol, immensely potent for all its non-existence – possibly the most potent image in the play. Symbolizing is an activity related to internal non-directional presences who seem to contain an ocean's depth. The turbulences of Noah's flood subside. The imaginative object is a consequence of the good object: both are examples of the potency which does not attack or enviously assault the helpless and enduring foetus-infant in myself.

17

The creation of the world

GOD'S WORLD is not the world of man's rebel-
lious mind; and when God reveals his world to
man, he challenges man's sanguine confidence in nature as a
mirror to the human soul. Man's myths about nature are
often myths about his own body, inclining (as he does) to see
his body and its appetites as the centre of being.

Genesis stands in the way of this assumption. It describes a
primal creation which is non-organic and in which there is no
biological coming-to-be or passing-away: no birth, no death
– and no nature. God might have articulated the idea of birth
and death to himself; but He did so in some way that was
only hinted at in the first pulse of creation. The fact that the
Creation occurs in time, and time is death-imbued, might, for
all its effect on the narrative, have been a liturgical after-
thought.

Creation's rhythm is linked to the time-span of a week,
discovering daily bread in the miraculous and sublimity in the
hearth. But it would be possible fairly to paraphrase the story
of primal creation without referring to this time-scheme.

The intellectual who organized the Priestly account of Genesis perhaps saw God in his own image – ascetic, celibate, in love with mathematical patterns and harmonies, opposed to organic fertility. The story of Noah's Ark might have been the product of the same imagination; it has the same aesthetic as well as structure as the Adam story. Both are stories of survival exercized through a universal economy of effect.

God could have started the human race with half a dozen Adams, a tribe – an infinity of primal fathers. But he did not. He made only one Adam. The vast company of the present world, its great number of individualisms, blinker man to the extent of human superfluity. At some time, it was otherwise. Long ago the world was parsimonious in its dispositions – but how long ago? Before the Fall; before the existence of Adam perhaps; or so Milton's Adam suggests, as he perplexedly contemplates the night sky:

> reasoning I oft admire
> How nature wise and frugal could commit
> Such disproportions, with superfluous hand
> So many nobler bodies to create
> (*Paradise Lost* 8:25–8)

Superfluity surfeits by its very superfluity and awakens the taste for sobriety. Aristotle imagined nature to be like a wise and frugal housewife: a pleasing simile – but one seldom supported by the evidence. The lovely spirals on a snail's shell do not seduce me into believing that nature is neat. Nature, as Aristotelian blueprint, is omnipotent conjecture – Adam becoming God and creating the world in the image of his own mathematician's mind. Enjoying the patterning in a fossil leaves undiminished the sense of the muddle in natural events; the spawn and blood of birth.

Why only one Adam, we ask. But then, why only one Noah? God decided to create only one man at the beginning of the world – and, coincidentally, it would seem – he finds only one man of virtue at the time of the Flood. The Old Testament God – the God of the priests, a God that the priests understand – is frugal, avoids duplication, has no liking for sub-plots, or for the nineteenth-century novelist's delight in dealing with awkward over-proliferated stories, mammoth families sighing and breathing their histories.

But the contributor to the Priestly version of Genesis is not writing a nineteenth-century novel. He is exploring a myth that is opposed to the enterprise of fiction – the myth of tales without tellers, impersonal and undeniable creations – anti-symbolist because anti-personality, foetal, conjoined to the surrounding substance. The author of Genesis is concerned to describe a minimal situation – the dialogue between God and the human self, the Adam in all men; and God requires only the minimum from mankind to maintain the dialogue: enough one Adam, one Noah.

But why need it be even one? Presumably because if all men had been drowned, the human race would have entered oblivion, and the stories of Adam and Noah lost to mind. The idea of mankind would have been separated from the idea of a tale without a teller. This would have continued to exist in a pre-symbolic realm of sky and sea and stars, in a sublime limbo, in actions too deep for thought.

Primal furnishings

How did the slippery wet world exist before human consciousness, at its first dawn; how did it continue to exist in the atmosphere of God? This is beyond my powers to understand. God exists outside consciousness, without the mediation of personality. God is sublime action. The frequent confirmations that his actions are good appear to be part of the rhythm of creation: moments of repose before the next creative surge.

Sir James Frazer refers to a Maori myth in which the divine Creator sees his creature as a reflection of himself. 'So like himself was the man whom the Maori Creator, Tiki, fashioned that he called him *Tiki-ahua*, that is, Tiki's likeness' (Frazer, 1916, vol. 1, p. 9). But the Genesis God does not lend himself to such a self-centredness. He is indistinguishable from the act of creation. He *is* the act of creation. The meaning of the act cannot be consciously or unconsciously thought about, since it cannot be dissociated from its maker, whose actions, like the actions of Lawrence's ego, exist beyond the actions of conscious thought.

Imagine the intellectual priest on board the Ark, drawing large inductions from minimal samples and writing up his poetry in tabernacle prose. He must have wondered whether the fabric of the world in first light was different from the fabric of the post-deluvial world, the olive branch in the dove's mouth a different essence from the first created things. But in their minimalist continuity, both kinds of object had something in common. They had to survive. The gopher-wood of the Ark – assuming it to be gopher-wood – was an essence that had to persist through cosmic transformations.

I would think that the first elements of the universe were objects, unique and unaffected by temporal process, finding no analogy in biological procreation, prototypes for such man-made things as tables and chairs. No one can propagate these prototypes and no one can destroy them, since they are ideas in the process of being incarnated, somatized thoughts; objects that have the attributes of ideas; ideas with some of the attributes of objects. But what are they exactly? Not hallucinations or hypochondriacal aches, although the unkind may think them so. Pre-birth conceptions perhaps, idea-objects, pre-symbolic entities, a necessary foundation for one mythic account of the world's beginnings. Object-ideas can only be made directly through God's fiat: light, darkness, day, night, the luminous orbs (possibly), the sky, the sea – they can only be made once; they have infinite power; and they are undeniable. Their awesome power lies in their being undeniable. (No idea of natural birth or miscarriage or death has come into being.)

By the fact of being object-ideas, they cannot be thought of as symbols or as having symbolic content. The act of being able to symbolize something presumes some capacity to separate objects and ideas. Object-ideas are hypothetical indicators of God's immortality; they are pre-symbolic and possibly pre-linguistic.

Diagrammatic

The Priestly account of creation at the very beginning of Genesis unfolds as impersonally as the definition of a theorem; it is diagrammatic. It implies a totality which can be divided and then divided again into increasing parts. 'In the beginning God created the heaven and the earth.' Earth and heaven are not greatly to be distinguished because they are both in darkness and without form – the creation of the waters is implicit in the makings of the earth.

'And God said, let there be light: and there was light.' The rhythm of creation hesitates, losing momentum with the making of light, as though the heavens had been temporarily exhausted. And then division occurs once again – quite abstractly, between light and darkness, day and night. The making of light precedes the making of the sun, the moon or the stars. In one deeply suggestive legend, God makes light, and then the light recedes; and in its receding, makes allowance for the first idea of space.

Oceans without seeming end, great grey wastes of water, the original element, binding acts of creation and destruction. Unceasing water at the Deluge also, sky water and subterranean water bursting their torn confines, the theme of water subsiding at the moment of the covenant, and re-surfacing in the Psalms. In the Babylonian Creation myths, the god Marduk makes the world through sub-division, by dismembering a female god or dragon or leviathan, Tiamat, who is identified with the sea. Some commentators think of Tiamat as an analogue to the Psalmist's Rahab, whom God hews to pieces.[1] The dismembering of the dragon-woman, Tiamat, the separating of water from water – like God's mysterious decision to divide the waters that were under the firmament from the waters above the firmament – uncovers an aggressive, even personalized intent in the notion of geometric division.

In the ur-texts, God is a dragon-slayer who slices up woman as a feared sexual being. But woman – she eventually appears in the Bible's apocalypse as the whore of Babylon – declines to be subdued. On the contrary, she distracts the bewildered mystics from their mathematical purity, as similarly, though less persecutedly, Eve wins Adam's heart from an absolute commitment to the non-biological godhead. The male ethos has been on the defensive ever since.

Within the totality, the divisions grow more and more minute, always containing within them the resonance of the totality. As the divisions decrease in size, the smallness of their particular parts increases. The poignancy of this procedure is such that we do not find ourselves asking about the exact nature of the relationship of the whole to its parts.

A universe without close detail: and yet the principle of division, once set in motion, by its direction implies the microscopic. The idea of continuously sub-dividing the totality into sections (beautifully proportioned to each other), carries within it the implication of the infinitely microscopic.

A physicist's rather than a biologist's universe, austere, non-organic, airless. A work-of-art universe, as imagined from within a room, faintly glowing through translucent walls; iconic, stylized trees and plants, tapestries, unfolding scrolls. A diagrammatic universe lending itself to geometric demonstration – in code.

The contract

Genesis begins – and continues as in its beginning – with an act of absolute creation that exists in an order of space and time that is not ours, self-generated, undivided and eternal: an act of a creation so total that it leaves space for nothing else.

The act of creation is inevitable in every part: nothing can be added to it or subtracted from it. No part can be got rid of because there is nowhere else for it to be got rid of into. If the totality were to disappear, we would lose everything. It is like the perfection of the sky, which I cannot add to or subtract from; it diminishes the sense I have of my own existence. I feel I have no place.

The making of the universe, complete in itself, is the beginning of the end – a tale that needs neither teller nor listener. I cannot stand it; I cannot think my way out of it; whatever way I turn, I find the fullest evidence of it. I want to make fictions, superfluities, all that God did not originally create: corsets and kettles, string quartets and Cubist paintings. True, it is the best of possible worlds, if only because I cannot myself conceive of any other. But – the voice of dissent says – God's absolute making of the world is a dead end. I admire the perfect sky. But what I admire is closed, in the sense that God made it utterly: why should God need me? Did my parents procreate me against God's wishes?

Mystery lies with the maker. Does the world, his reflection, carry the mystery? Each part carries the resonance of the totality within itself. Its integrity is monistic – and disconnected from modern intuition. In Genesis, pluralism is the enemy, devil-inspired, probably related to ancestor worship and the creation of images. Monism is revelatory in effect; pluralism is not. Pluralism is piecemeal. The Genesis scribes think of pluralistic enterprises as catastrophic: towers fall, nations scatter and tongues proliferate.

Note

1 'Thou rulest the raging of the sea: when the waves thereof arise thou stillest them. Thou hast broken Rahab in pieces, as one that is slain; thou hast scattered thine enemies with thy strong arm' (Psalm 89:9–10).

18

Adam in generation

GENESIS DOES not indicate that Adam dreamt during his deep sleep; and this is significant, since it is important to imagine Adam's sleep as being a sleep without mind, a stupor that exists where mind one day might be. However, if I think of Adam as a prototype for the other patriarchs, whom I know to have been dreamers, then I feel some inclination to follow Milton and to think that Adam dreamt in his deep sleep.

Abraham's dream, Joseph's dream and the possible dream that Noah dreamt when God advised him to build an Ark, are dreams of survival, continuation, making new – commentaries on the dream that Milton was much later to ascribe to his post-Renaissance and Anglicized hero. In all these cases, the primal act of creation – God as *natura naturans* – appears to the dreamer and offers a pledge: the present will continue into the future. The prospects of food and of breath will not cease. Life will continue beyond the next harvest.

In Milton's version, the dream of continuity is of a woman

– Eve – who realizes the future for Adam, in ways that God presumably had not planned. In one form or another, the source of life, of primal creativity itself, validates a depth of seriousness in the dreamer that the dreamer finds awesome, even overwhelming. This Adam is not like Jacob at Bethel; he does not directly dream of God. He dreams of God's creativity in a form that is not immediately God-like. A fragment of actuality first appears to him in a dream, as though it were a piece of sky, or a star – one of the primal furnishings of the universe. He awakes and finds its truth. Eve, as a realized being, is truth: the source of poetry.

God accommodates the creation to Adam's needs. From now on, in the human sphere, God will abandon direct creativity; he will delegate creativity to the human couple. And this will bring about changes in the aesthetic of the world. God's creation had been minimalist, economic, its objects unique. Now creation will be duplicative, without end, and without seeming order. Adam's dreaming of Eve at the moment in which God transforms her out of a piece of God's body marks the point in transition. Indeed, dreaming up the existence of a person at the moment when they are born in actuality is a supremely foolish and beautiful example of human superfluity in creation.

In comparison, God practises the economy of a frugal artist. He does not make Eve as an adjunct to the created universe. He takes her from a part of Adam's body. He re-uses a bit of matter – Adam's rib – to re-furbish the old. Against divine spareness, human proliferation. Is this the moment when a human symbolism comes into being?

Adam, pregnant with Eve, swoons as though dying at the moment of birth. He comes to some awareness of having an inside, spiritual as well as physical. He becomes aware of the possibility of internalizing other beings – as figures in his mind. The father who studied his son's X-ray with intense concern, seemed benevolently to sanction his son's future existence – or so his son was later able to feel. The father's goodness was related to the father's intimate knowledge of the foetal self, or soul, that continuously exists in the no man's land between life and death. The father was a healer. And so too with the Eve-foetus. She puts Adam in touch with a soul or foetal self that he had never known – and with a sense of the future, so strengthening of his courage that she and he can risk the voyage through death in the hours of birth.

Granted the mother's function, Adam is not allowed to witness Eve's emergence from his body. God is the obstetrician: and yet, however dissociatedly, Adam gives birth to her. God made him out of dust; he, as God's agent, gives birth to Eve out of bone. A wife springs up from his insides; and he loves her as he might a newborn infant. It is the first act of human birth on record – and the only known case of a male parturition.

In giving birth to Eve, he not only allows her a life of her own, he relinquishes the procreative function in its entirety; as previously God had relinquished the procreative function a little in allowing him to give birth to Eve. The direct line between creator and his creation has been broken. The world no longer reflects God face to face: and the prime revelation of the Bible has been distanced. Adam, having given birth once, must lose the intimacy of direct potency. He will become an agent for the seed and no more. Procreation moves into someone else. (And this will be the fate of those who follow him. No human being, whether female or male, has a direct sense of creating the future. It is always our mothers who give birth, never ourselves as daughters, and our mothers are like the tomorrows that are always to come: we can never appropriate their powers. We are at most agents to the creations of others.)

From now on, Adam's femininity can only manifest itself through thought, as it had been previously so in the act of naming the animals. Naming, using speech, being a poet, is a consolatory form of parturition. God invites a hard-working vegetarian gardener to exercise the powers of language, relinquishing divine authority over language, in the same way as Adam will later relinquish biological aptitudes to his wife.

In observing the animals and in naming them, Adam takes nature into his heart. (We do not know in what tongue he spoke.)

A new order emerges which disturbs the cocooning love of God and Adam. Adam gives birth to God's daughter, and his desire for his daughter-wife, mysterious and ever-ramifying personality, finds its natural outlet in the family: communities of storytellers and listeners, resonators of feeling. The monistic world of the womb gives way to the larger uterine composure of the family. Adam and Eve discover a human bias: the desire to be like the ant and to multiply.

Asserting their independence of the covenant, making their precarious and often luxurious fictions, our beautiful ancestors fought the fear that faces anyone who looks into the sky and cannot bear its perfection. Perfection is authorless; and a tale without a teller is a tale that needs no listener. The sky informs me that I have no necessary place in this lovely world. Human aspiration is inhibited by the perfection of a world that greets it at first and last sight. Human fictions are precarious; and it is tempting to use the idea of the family to strengthen fictions against the coming deluge.

God's pre-symbolic makings existed outside the workings of mind. Through Adam's act of birth in sleep, mankind discovers the birth of symbolic expression. Symbolic expression, like fiction, is uncertain. In dream, the future generations of Adam are provisionally foreshadowed. The future generations rise from the dust like guards to protect the transient manufacturings of the human spirit.

The generations of Adam mark the divisions of Adam – the disintegration of mankind into individual selves. Impersonal and recurrent narratives, the unconscious sway of life and death within, continue to threaten the human association. The tale without teller will not go away.

Unpent river

Two among the many aspects of woman: the idealized artist's model who inspires men to discover sublime structures,

Adam giving birth to idealized woman out of his insides; or woman in dialogue with the biological cycle of birth and death and in touch with the actual stuffs of bodies – flesh, viscera, bones, viscous fluids; the woman that Aristotle is honest enough to admit to finding distasteful and at the same time to think the only site of scientific knowledge (Aristotle, 1912, 1.5.645a). Eve in her second aspect intimates mortality, the passing-away as well as the coming-to-be of bodies: she is the Eve who fosters original sin, a concept whose range includes (Augustine thought) the sufferings of disease and death as well as of mortal error. Original sin is body bias – in Augustine, a bias increasing with each generation.

Eve brings me to an awareness of superfluity. In time, we shall all be redundant. We are not the first; and it is hard to regain the idea of a meaningful primal experience. Many have lived before us. Most lives have ended; an infinitesimal number of them are registered in contemporary consciousness. Many lives have hardly been forgotten – they have never been known.

To avoid this thought, I want to move back in time, to its very beginning, to the primal parents: here there is uniqueness, freshness and no loss. Nothing stales or goes bad or is evacuated. (And nothing is born or dies.) I want to emphasize the chastity of first impression.

When someone I love dies, I am liable to feel a surge of grief at the thought that this is the first day in which the sun has not shone on the dead one in many years. Straight after a death, time moves forward suddenly and with unexpected speed surges forward, carrying before it superfluities, like twigs on an unpent river.

At the first moment, nothing is born and nothing dies. And in a strange way, nothing matters. The mystery is this: in the post-creationist world, where things just happen, I feel superfluous – until I find myself witness to a death or birth. And then I realize that every individual is precious beyond human valuation. I think to come to truth. I suspect that this was the implied meaning of Adam's dream.

First love

God has the capacity to predict the unpredictable. He understands Adam's need for a help-meet and he has the incomparable imaginative ability to matchmake Adam with a type of being who does not as yet exist.

Adam thinks Eve is unique: this is the nature of his love. He does not think of her as single, isolated or alone (which would make a nonsense of thinking her unique). She is a unique figure in an imagined civilization of women. Adam is drawn to her as though as of choice, as though she were one among many, and he celebrates her as though in congregation. The poignancy of this first and possibly greatest human love was that it was not pre-ordained. In Milton, if not in Genesis, God decided that Adam should be an individual and acquire a mind.

Eve, in her uniqueness, begins the biological cycle, in which there is a coming-to-be and a passing-away. Mankind enters into a great loneliness. Individuals join hands across the generations. They enter into communities. They converse with each other. The waters of the sea rise up. The realm of the tales without tellers is restricted. Only at times of great catastrophe – as at times of a world war – will it be recollected (by D. H. Lawrence, among others).

The sublime leads to the relatively ridiculous: the Fall of Man marks the Rise of Literature and the Beginnings of History. Ancestors come into being, family stories, tellers of tales and their listeners – and with them, of course, arrives the greatest stimulus to story-telling, the jesting figures of Death and Birth.

Bibliography

Allen, D. C. (1949) *The Legend of Noah*. Illinois.

Aquinas, T. (1964) *Summa Theologiae*, vol. 4, *Knowledge in God*. London.

Aristotle (1912) *The Parts of the Animals*, W. Ogle, trans. Oxford.

Bettelheim, B. (1987) *A Good Enough Parent*. London.

Browne, T. (1643) *Religio Medici*. Menston, 1970.

——(1984) *The Major Works*, C. A. Patrides, ed. London.

Bunyan, J. (1666) *Grace Abounding to the Chief of Sinners*, Roger Sharrock, ed. Oxford, 1962.

Cassirer, E. (1950) *The Philosophy of Symbolic Forms*, vol. 2, *Mythical Thought*. New Haven, CT.

Coleridge, S. T. (1817) *Biographia Literaria*, George Watson, ed. London.

——(1981) *Marginalia*, G. Walley, ed., vol. 1. Princeton, NJ.

Eliade, M. (1957) *Myths, Dreams and Mysteries*. London.

Eliot, T. S. (1944) *Four Quartets*. London.

Empson, W. (1961) *Milton's God*. London.

The Epic of Gilgamesh (1972) N. K. Saunders, trans. London.

Evans, A. (1901) *The Mycenean Tree and Pillar Cult*. London.

Evans-Wentz, W. Y. (1949) *The Tibetan Book of the Dead*. Oxford.

Forman, M. B., ed. (1935) *The Letters of John Keats*. Oxford, 1952.

Frazer, J. G. (1916) *Folk-Lore in the Old Testament*. London, 2nd edn, 1919.

Frye, N. (1947) *Fearful Symmetry. A Study of William Blake*. Princeton, NJ, 1962.

Gibson, M. D., ed. (1901) 'Apocrypha Arabica' in *Studia Sinaitica* VIII(1) *The Book of the Rolls*. London.

Graves, R. (1948) *Collected Poems*. London.

Huxley, A., ed. (1950) *D. H. Lawrence. Letters*, selected by Richard Aldington. Harmondsworth.

Jammer, M. (1954) *Concepts of Space*. Cambridge, MA.

King, L. W. (1918) *Legends of Babylon and Egypt in Relation to Hebrew Tradition*. London.

Koyré, A. (1968) *Metaphysics and Measurement*. London.

Lawrence, D. H. (1934) *The Tales of D. H. Lawrence*. London, 1948.

——(1957) *The Complete Poems* (3 vols). London.

Lévi-Bruhl, L. (1936) *Primitives and the Supernatural*. London.

Lévi-Strauss, C. (1964) *The Raw and the Cooked*. London, 1970.

Lovejoy, A. and Boas, M. (1935) *Primitivism and Related Ideas in Antiquity*. New York.

Milton, J. (1971) *Complete Prose Works*, vol. 5. New Haven, CT.

Moore, T. H., ed. (1962) *The Collected Letters of D. H. Lawrence*, vol. 1. London.

Nuttall, G. F. (1946) *The Holy Spirit in Puritan Faith and Experience*. Oxford.

Peirce, C. S. (1931) *Collected Papers*, vol. 1, *Principles of Philosophy*. Cambridge, MA.

Plotinus (1984) *Enneads 4. 1–9*. A. H. Armstrong, trans. Cambridge, MA.

Poe, E. A. (1899) *The Works of Edgar Allan Poe*, John H. Ingram, ed. London.

Proust, M. (1958) *By Way of Sainte-Beuve*. London.

Rubin, W. (1984) *'Primitivism' in 20th Century Art*. New York.

Santayana, G. (1896) *The Sense of Beauty*. New York.

Schofield, J. N. (1938) *The Historical Background of the Bible*. London.

Sibbes, R. (1863) *Works*, A. B. Grosast, ed. London.

Tolstoy, L. (1886) *The Death of Ivan Ilyich*. Harmondsworth, 1960.

Tylor, E. B. (1871) *Primitive Culture*. London.

Van Gennep, A. (1960) *The Rites of Passage*. H. B. Vizedom and G. L. Caffee, trans. London.

Von Rad, G. (1970) *Genesis: A Commentary*. London.

Watkins, O. C. (1972) *The Puritan Experience*. London.

Wellhausen, J. (1885) *Prolegomena to the History of Israel*. Edinburgh.

Westermann, C. (1984) *Genesis 1–11: A Commentary*. London.

Williams, N. P. (1927) *The Ideas of the Fall and of Original Sin*. London.

Wolfson, H. A. (1947) *Philo*, 2 vols. Cambridge, MA.

Index

This first edition of
The Generations of Adam
was finished in October 1990.

It was set in 11/14 Sabon
on a Linotron 202
printed on a web-offset press

The book was commissioned and
edited by Karl Figlio,
designed by David Mann,
indexed by Sue Ramsey
and produced by Miranda Chaytor
for Free Association Books.